✧ *Companions for the Journey* ✧

Praying with
C. S. Lewis

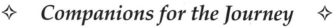
Companions for the Journey

Praying with
C. S. Lewis

by
Charles C. Taliaferro

Saint Mary's Press
Christian Brothers Publications
Winona, Minnesota

Genuine recycled paper with 10% post-consumer waste.
Printed with soy-based ink.

The publishing team for this book included Carl Koch, series editor; Rosemary Broughton, development editor; Laurie A. Berg, copy editor; James H. Gurley, production editor and typesetter; Cindi Ramm, cover designer; Maurine R. Twait, art director; Elaine Kohner, illustrator; pre-press, printing, and binding by the graphics division of Saint Mary's Press.

The acknowledgments continue on page 113.

Printed in the United States of America

Printing: 9 8 7 6 5 4 3 2 1

Year: 2006 05 04 03 02 01 00 99 98

ISBN 0-88489-318-9

✧ Contents ✧

✧ Foreword ✧

Companions for the Journey

Just as food is required for human life, so are companions. Indeed, the word *companions* comes from two Latin words: *com*, meaning "with," and *panis*, meaning "bread." Companions nourish our heart, mind, soul, and body. They are also the people with whom we can celebrate the sharing of bread.

Perhaps the most touching stories in the Bible are about companionship: the Last Supper, the wedding feast at Cana, the sharing of the loaves and the fishes, and Jesus' breaking of bread with the disciples on the road to Emmaus. Each incident of companionship with Jesus revealed more about his mercy, love, wisdom, suffering, and hope. When Jesus went to pray in the Garden of Olives, he craved the companionship of the Apostles. They let him down. But God sent the Spirit to inflame the hearts of the Apostles, and they became faithful companions to Jesus and to one another.

Throughout history, other faithful companions have followed Jesus and the Apostles. These saints and mystics have also taken the journey from conversion, through suffering, to resurrection. Just as they were inspired by the holy people who went before them, so too may you be inspired by these saints and mystics and take them as your companions on your spiritual journey.

The Companions for the Journey series is a response to the spiritual hunger of Christians. This series makes available the rich spiritual teachings of mystics and guides whose wisdom can help us on our pilgrimage. As you complete the last meditation in each volume, it is hoped that you will feel supported, challenged, and affirmed by a soul-companion on your spiritual journey.

The spiritual hunger that has emerged over the last twenty years is a great sign of renewal in Christian life. People fill retreat programs and workshops on topics in spirituality. The demand for spiritual directors exceeds the number available. Interest in the lives and writings of saints and mystics is increasing as people search for models of whole and holy Christian life.

Praying with C. S. Lewis

Praying with C. S. Lewis is more than just a book about Lewis's spirituality. This book seeks to engage you in praying in the way that Lewis did about issues and themes that were central to his experience. Each meditation can enlighten your understanding of his spirituality and lead you to reflect on your own experience.

The goal of *Praying with C. S. Lewis* is that you will discover Lewis's rich spirituality and integrate his spirit and wisdom into your relationship with God, with your brothers and sisters, and with your own heart and mind.

Suggestions for Praying with C. S. Lewis

Meet C. S. Lewis, a fascinating companion for your pilgrimage, by reading the introduction to this book. It provides a brief biography of Lewis and an outline of the major themes of his spirituality.

Once you meet C. S. Lewis, you will be ready to pray with him and to encounter God, your sisters and brothers, and yourself in new and wonderful ways. To help your prayer, here are some suggestions that have been part of the tradition of Christian spirituality:

Create a sacred space. Jesus said, "'Whenever you pray, go into your room and shut the door and pray to your [God] who is in secret; and your [God] who sees in secret will reward you'" (Matthew 6:6). Solitary prayer is best done in a place where you can have privacy and silence, both of which can be luxuries in the life of busy people. If privacy and silence are not possible, create a quiet, safe place within yourself, perhaps while riding to and from work, while sitting in line at the dentist's office, or while waiting for someone. Do the best you can, knowing that a loving God is present everywhere. Whether the meditations in this book are used for solitary prayer or with a group, try to create a prayerful mood with candles, meditative music, an open Bible, or a crucifix.

Open yourself to the power of prayer. Every human experience has a religious dimension. All of life is suffused with God's presence. So remind yourself that God is present as you begin your period of prayer. Do not worry about distractions. If something keeps intruding during your prayer, spend some time talking with God about it. Be flexible because God's spirit blows where it will.

Prayer can open your mind and widen your vision. Be open to new ways of seeing God, people, and yourself. As you open yourself to the spirit of God, different emotions are evoked, such as sadness from tender memories, or joy from a celebration recalled. Our emotions are messages from God that can tell us much about our spiritual quest. Also, prayer strengthens our will to act. Through prayer, God can touch our will and empower us to live according to what we know is true.

Finally, many of the meditations in this book will call you to employ your memories, your imagination, and the circumstances of your life as subjects for prayer. The great mystics and saints realized that they had to use all their resources to know God better. Indeed, God speaks to us continually and touches us constantly. We must learn to listen and feel with all the means that God has given us.

Come to prayer with an open mind, heart, and will.

Preview each meditation before beginning. After you have placed yourself in God's presence, spend a few moments previewing the readings and especially the reflection activities. Several reflection activities are given in each meditation because different styles of prayer appeal to different personalities or personal needs. **Note that each meditation has more reflection activities than can be done during one prayer period. Therefore, select only one or two reflection activities each time you use a meditation. Do not feel compelled to complete all the reflection activities.**

Read meditatively. Each meditation offers you a story about Lewis and a reading from his writings. Take your time reading. If a particular phrase touches you, stay with it. Relish its feelings, meanings, and concerns.

Use the reflections. Following the readings is a short reflection in commentary form, which is meant to give perspective to the readings. Then you are offered several ways of meditating on the readings and the theme of the prayer. You may be familiar with the different methods of meditating, but in case you are not, they are described briefly here:

✦ *Repeated short prayer or mantra:* One means of focusing your prayer is to use a *mantra*, or "prayer word." The mantra may be a single word or a short phrase taken from the readings or from the Scriptures. For example, a short prayer for meditation 1 in this book might simply be "Begin where you are." Repeated slowly in harmony with your breathing, the mantra helps you center your heart and mind on one action or attribute of God.

✦ *Lectio divina:* This type of meditation is "divine studying," a concentrated reflection on the word of God or the wisdom of a spiritual writer. Most often in *lectio divina*, you will be invited to read one of the passages several times and then concentrate on one or two sentences, pondering their meaning for you and their effect on you. *Lectio divina* commonly ends with formulation of a resolution.

✦ *Guided meditation:* In this type of meditation, our imagination helps us consider alternative actions and likely consequences. Our imagination helps us experience new ways of seeing God, our neighbors, ourselves, and nature. When Jesus told his followers parables and stories, he engaged their imagination. In this book, you will be invited to follow guided meditations.

One way of doing a guided meditation is to read the scene or story several times, until you know the outline and can recall it when you enter into reflection. Or before your prayer time, you may wish to record the meditation on a tape recorder. If so, remember to allow pauses for reflection between phrases and to speak with a slow, peaceful pace and tone. Then, during prayer, when you have finished the readings and the reflection commentary, you can turn on your recording of the meditation and be led through it. If you find your own voice too distracting, ask a friend to make the tape for you.

✦ *Examen of consciousness:* The reflections often will ask you to examine how God has been speaking to you in your past and present experience—in other words, the reflections will ask you to examine your awareness of God's presence in your life.

✦ *Journal writing:* Writing is a process of discovery. If you write for any length of time, stating honestly what is on your mind and in your heart, you will unearth much about who you are, how you stand with your God, what deep longings reside in your soul, and more. In some reflections, you will be asked to write a dialog with Jesus or someone else. If you have never used writing as a means of meditation, try it. Reserve a special notebook for your journal writing. If desired, you can go back to your entries at a future time for an examen of consciousness.

✦ *Action:* Occasionally, a reflection will suggest singing a favorite hymn, going out for a walk, or undertaking some other physical activity. Actions can be meaningful forms of prayer.

Using the Meditations for Group Prayer

If you wish to use the meditations for community prayer, these suggestions may help:

✦ Read the theme to the group. Call the community into the presence of God, using the short opening prayer. Invite one or two participants to read one or both readings. If you use both readings, observe the pause between them.

✦ The reflection commentary may be used as a reading, or it can be deleted, depending on the needs and interests of the group.

✦ Select one of the reflection activities for your group. Allow sufficient time for your group to reflect, to recite a centering prayer or mantra, to accomplish a studying prayer *(lectio divina)*, or to finish an examen of consciousness. Depending on the group and the amount of available time, you may want to invite the participants to share their reflections, responses, or petitions with the group.

✦ Reading the passage from the Scriptures may serve as a summary of the meditation.

✦ If a formulated prayer or a psalm is given as a closing, it may be recited by the entire group. Or you may ask participants to offer their own prayers for the closing.

Now you are ready to begin praying with C. S. Lewis, a faithful and caring companion on this stage of your spiritual journey. It is hoped that you will find him to be a true soul-companion.

CARL KOCH
Editor

✧ **Preface** ✧

I take great delight in the opportunity to share these meditations and reflections. I believe the work of C. S. Lewis is especially well suited to this series, given the central place in his life Lewis gave to companionship. In a collection of reminiscences about C. S. Lewis, a friend reports: "He was the greatest man I have ever known. Perhaps what has endeared him to me most, he was the best of companions" (James T. Como, ed., *C. S. Lewis at the Breakfast Table and Other Reminiscences*, p. 125). Lewis was not vain, so I imagine he would have been uneasy about being singled out as the greatest or the best, but I believe he would have been overjoyed to be called a good companion. Lewis's own writings and the testimony of those who knew him well provide abundant evidence that he treasured companionship and friendship. Lewis wholeheartedly engaged in the rites of companionship, whether these involved the sharing of pleasures or the shouldering of burdens.

I did not know Lewis personally as a teacher-companion, but his work has had a tremendous influence on me over almost thirty years. He has stood out for me as a model teacher and scholar, as well as spiritual guide. I therefore feel a special honor in being asked by Ben Nagel, a former student at Saint Olaf College, to write this book. As a college teacher, I have had ample occasion to note the ways in which students refer to their teachers. Sometimes students say that they have taken a class with a professor; alternatively they will say that they are students of a professor or that they studied under a professor. In North American higher education today, we are unlikely to find too many uses of the latter expression because it suggests subservience. Today we often emphasize a partnership in education involving both teacher and student. I think this is altogether desirable, and this is my own preferred understanding of teaching, but I should have been happy if I could report that I had studied under C. S. Lewis. His wonderful combination of imagination and intelligence in a God-centered life has been a deep inspiration for his students and for so many of those who knew him personally. Through Lewis's many books and letters, and through accounts of his life, I have sought to join those who studied under him. I now offer for your consideration these meditations that have taken shape over the years, in the hope that you will be stimulated to go to Lewis's works and to the works of those who inspired him, as well as to those whom he inspired, in order to continue the journey that is sketched in the pages that follow.

I am very grateful to Carl Koch and Rosemary Broughton for their encouragement, editing, and contributions, especially to the section of each chapter on spiritual exercises. I thank Dorothy Bolton and Kimberly Ronning for invaluable assistance in preparing the manuscript, and William Narum, an esteemed colleague who has blessed Saint Olaf with Lewis's spirit for many years. This book is written with love and in special gratitude for Barclay, Bonnie, Carol Lynn, Eric, Eliza, Elizabeth, Father Francisco, Gayle, John, James, Katie, Kris, Larry, Laurel, Leigh, Marianne, Meg, Michel, Nancy, Philip, Rick, Todd, and Tomas. This is also written with great affection and devotion for James and Karen Evans. May each reader be upheld by such dear friends! I also write in appreciation for the C. S. Lewis Society and its kind hospitality during Trinity Term 1992 at Oxford, England.

✧ Introduction ✧

For most of his life, C. S. Lewis was a don at Oxford University and then at Cambridge University. When asked what a don did, he replied:

> Taking "tutorials" occupies the best part of his day, i.e., pupils come in pairs, read essays to him, then follows criticism, discussion, etc.; then he gives public lectures on his own subject; takes his share in the business of managing the College; prepares his lectures and writes books; and in his spare time stands in queues. (W. H. Lewis, ed., *Letters of C. S. Lewis*, p. 214)

Clive Staples Lewis was a don, but he was so much more. From the outside his life may seem uncomplicated, ordered, tranquil. But Lewis's life was rich; and his experience, love, and devotion to God in prayer were profound and dramatic.

Indeed, Lewis was a soldier in World War I. In the years following, he went on to become a world-renowned scholar in medieval and Renaissance studies at two of the most prestigious universities in the English-speaking world. He wrote as a novelist, a poet, an essayist, a children's story writer, and even as an author of science fiction books. He was equally adept at analyzing intricate ancient texts, explaining the medieval worldview, engaging in serious intellectual debate about the relationship between science and religion, and writing playful stories about myth, magic, and fantasy. From the 1930s on, C. S. Lewis was among the most gifted, sensitive, and eloquent defenders of prayer and Christian spirituality. He courageously embraced and defended Christianity at a time when skepticism, existentialism, atheism, and rationalism permeated the intellectual and cultural climate.

Fullness of Life

Lewis's spirituality—indeed his whole philosophy of life—is a fascinating configuration of unity and diversity. His spirituality is unified insofar as God is acknowledged as the divine Trinity who creates and conserves the cosmos in being, the God in whom and by whom all things are redeemed, and the final end and ultimate goal of all values. Putting his position in very simple, stark terms, Lewis proposed that "to walk out of [God's] will is to walk into nowhere" (C. S. Lewis, *Perelandra*, p. 116).

Yet, despite his extraordinarily unified outlook and belief, Lewis relished the complex, many-layers of life. The overriding unity of God's reality did not for an instant eclipse or compromise the vast expanse of natural goods or the rich breadth of human activity. The Incarnation of God in Christ grounded the many ways in which human loss may be recovered or transformed. While affirming that God is the highest good, Lewis also recognized the awesome plenitude of goods in the natural order of creation. In brief, Lewis's spirituality was built around a vision of the fullness of life in God.

Lewis's philosophy of the unity of life in God and the diversity of life in creation took shape in his study of desire and human longing. In his exploration of ancient, medieval, and modern literature, Lewis focused on the yearning for fulfillment. Today we may readily list a host of desires for fulfillment that are at play in our own era, ranging from the commonplace to the exotic: a child's desire for parental love; a romantic's desire for erotic bliss; an adult's desire for friendship, gain, power, and a healthy life. Not every human desire is for a true good, of course, and yet Lewis sought to chart and honor the restless desire for what is believed to be good. Lewis thought that the deepest of desires for human well-being and for the happiness of others are hints of a greater landscape, or world, in which desire and indeed human nature itself can find fulfillment.

If Lewis is right, then in the end, our sustained longing for fulfillment and fruition cannot be met in the horizon or with the resources of this world alone. Humans have a need for the God beyond the frontiers of nature in whom can be found fullness of life. We may or may not explicitly recognize that our deepest longings are tied in with a yearning for a living relationship with God, but an integrated divine-human relation is, in Lewis's view, the appropriate end of human passion and life. "The human soul was made to enjoy some object that is never fully given—nay, cannot even be imagined as given—in our present mode of subjective and spatio-temporal experience" (C. S. Lewis, *The Pilgrim's Regress*, p. 10).

In Lewis's vision of the kindling of desire and the ultimate fulfillment of human longing, he carefully highlights the integrity of each element. According to Lewis, human desires for natural goods—justice, friendship, family, romantic love, knowledge, the flourishing of personal talent—are not meant to be extinguished by an all-absorbing, passion for God. They are meant to be ordered, and thus their fruition enjoyed.

The key to this integrated fulfillment lies in the supple, courteous, and artful way in which God animates and illuminates human life. God calls us into fulfillment both in relation with one another and in relation to God. In traditional theological language, God is the highest good, but in creation are multiple diverse goods. It is in virtue of the good that desires should be seen and forged. When passions and desires are tyrannical, destructive, and in lethal conflict with one another, they are to be set right, not so much out of disgust with evil as out of love for a richer, higher good.

Lewis's thinking was very much along the lines of Saint Augustine's on this point: it is delight that should order the soul. A healthy life is one in which there is an *ordo amoris*, a divine order of love. Wickedness is to be rejected because, in the end, it is not a food but a poison. It cannot nourish us; it saps our native strength. Wickedness tends to collapse and destroy the goods of creation, whereas a God-centered life stabilizes, honors, and elevates the goods of our world.

A Divine Desire

Lewis's philosophy of desire and its ultimate satisfaction may appear to some as a colossal case of wish fulfillment, a quick, easy, and simplistic course in self-satisfaction. As it happens, Lewis's reasons for believing that a God exists who fulfills human desire are extensive and articulate, and they involve more than, "I desire fulfillment, therefore God exists." The bracing and provocative contribution by Lewis is that he challenges the cynicism, despair, and suspicion that can so easily pervade contemporary life. Rather than being victims of wish fulfillment, today many are more likely to fall prey to its opposite, to disbelieve some message or dimension of reality because "it is too good to be true." The import of much of Lewis's work is that it throws human desire and yearning into a new light. The yearning for a fulfillment that cannot be fully realized in this world raises a deep question about the very limits of the world. Lewis did not want any of his students or readers to be gullible and believe in a kind of fantastic mix of false hope and euphoric mysticism. Even so, he was keen to challenge the prevalent business-as-usual skepticism. Lewis's message is for his listeners to be attentive to the world as they sensately, emotionally, and rationally experience it. He challenges them to be open to the possibility of a larger landscape where they may find themselves and all their relationships swept up into a greater drama in which God is the author, the producer, and the key point of reference.

Lewis believed that meditation and prayer constitute a vital place in which to encounter this God of life, the God who calls us to take seriously the deepest levels of our identity and desire. Prayer and meditation are no mere tools for natural solitary introspection, or secondary and minor decorations for a well-lived life. Prayer and meditation are major activities that mediate and expand our familiar world of thought, feeling, desire, and sensation. The single verse from the Christian Bible that speaks with distinctive clarity and force to Lewis's position is the statement of Jesus found in the fourth Gospel, "'I came that they may have life, and have it abundantly'" (John 10:10). In Lewis's view, prayer and meditation are pivotal in the cultivation of such abundance. Prayer and meditation form a place where our ordinary thoughts and desires can be transformed in an extraordinary way in relation to God.

In Lewis's life, the role of prayer and meditation is manifest in his work as an author and scholar, in his reflections on his battlefield experience in World War I, in the joys and sorrow of his marriage, and in the pleasures of friendship and collegiality at Oxford and later at Cambridge universities.

Jack

Clive Staples Lewis was born in 1898 in Belfast, Ireland. At the age of four, he announced to his family that from then on he was "Jacksie," which, as he grew up, became "Jack."

Jack and his brother, Warren, were fast friends, and they roamed County Down on their bicycles; composed stories in the attic of Little Lea, their large house; and read voraciously. Even as a child, Lewis made up stories that his father would write down for him.

Lewis was brought up as a Christian, but his early religious training was piecemeal and soon gave way to a thoroughgoing skepticism. When his mother became seriously ill, Lewis prayed that God would save her. When she died in 1908, Lewis turned away from the God who had let him down.

His experiences in boarding schools—Wynyard, Campbell College, Cherbourg House, Malvern College—did little to change Lewis's opinion about God. As a young man, Lewis thought of Christianity as simply one myth among many other myths. In his youthful opinion, Christianity happened to survive the ancient world, but it was no more credible than its now extinct Near East counterparts.

At the time of Lewis's university education, the English-speaking world was fast becoming aware of the staggering number of divine beings postulated by ancient people. In the wake of such a mammoth overpopulation of gods, why should anyone think the Christian God was anything more than simply a lucky myth, a relic, or at best a souvenir from a superstitious past?

Religious skepticism was Lewis's considered view as he began studies at Oxford University in 1917. Soon the army recruited him to serve in World War I. The horror of war led him to feel that his skepticism was confirmed. He was a second lieutenant in the Somerset Light Infantry, on the front line in

France, and he was wounded in action at Mount Bernenchon in 1918.

Lewis also lost his friend Paddy Moore, his roommate at Keble College, Oxford. When Paddy was killed, Lewis assumed a son's role in the life of Paddy's mother. Mrs. Moore and Paddy's sister, Maureen, became a second family for Lewis. When he established his home at the Kilns in Oxford, he invited Mrs. Moore to live with him. She did so until her death in 1951.

Myth and Fact

Army duty done, Lewis finished his studies at Oxford over the next few years. In 1924, he became a tutor at University College, Oxford, a position he held until 1954, and then a fellow at Magdalene College. Lewis distinguished himself as one of the bright lights of his day in literary and historical criticism. He was, in effect, a philosophy major, who then used his philosophical skills in his literary studies.

Like all faculty Lewis had rooms at the college where he tutored and a home off campus, too. Most days Lewis would walk the three miles home to the Kilns (named because kilns to make bricks still stood near the house) for lunch and a walk with his dogs. If the weather permitted, Lewis would take a swim in the pond on the grounds. Indeed, Lewis took great delight in both hiking and swimming. For the most part, life settled into a productive rhythm for Lewis, but still a large area of discontent nagged him: the difficulty of consistently denying the existence of God.

Lewis's conversion to Christianity was not an all-at-once affair, and it may be traced through many relationships and conversations from 1923 to 1931, especially his exchanges with J. R. R. Tolkien and Hugo Dyson.

At first Lewis became disillusioned with the antireligious philosophy of his time. It became less and less obvious to Lewis that our vastly complex, ordered cosmos, replete with intelligent, conscious, moral life, was simply an accident or an effect of mindless laws of nature. The order and continued existence of the cosmos did not appear to be self-explaining, and if there was no God, the existence of our strong moral convictions seemed to Lewis to be baffling and ungrounded.

Lewis was convinced of the existence of good and evil—the bloodshed of World War I confirmed for him the existence of evil in merciless terms—and he began to entertain questions about whether objective values of good and evil could be merely natural creations, the outcome of evolution for example. Is it only a natural and mutable fact that cruelty is wrong, or does such a moral fact reflect the character and judgment of something beyond this natural and historical world?

> My argument against God was that the universe seemed so cruel and unjust. But how had I got this idea of *just* and *unjust?* A man does not call a line crooked unless he has some idea of a straight line. What was I comparing this universe with when I called it unjust? If the whole show was bad and senseless from A to Z, so to speak, why did I, who was supposed to be part of the show, find myself in such violent reaction against it? . . . Thus in the very act of trying to prove that God did not exist—in other words, that the whole of reality was senseless—I found I was forced to assume that one part of reality —namely my idea of justice—was full of sense. Consequently atheism turns out to be too simple. If the whole universe has no meaning, we should never have found out that it has no meaning. (C. S. Lewis, *Mere Christianity,* p. 31)

In Lewis's view, moral experience suggests a reality and a standard of judgment that are greater than human invention.

At the same time that Lewis began to question the confident naturalism of his day, he rethought the dismissal of religious experience. There were, indeed, many different religions. But does this fact serve the case for religious skepticism? Cannot a person interpret the many reports of humankind to have experienced some divine reality as providing evidence, however modest, that some kind of divine reality exists? A hundred people may describe a wedding a hundred different ways, and we may find it difficult to decide which account is the best, but the many different reports, taken together, count as evidence that a wedding did indeed take place. Lewis also pondered that in our own time we hear abundant testimony by vast numbers of people across widely diverse cultures of experiencing a divine reality. Many of these people seem to be otherwise mature, intelligent, ethical, and honest. Perhaps the wide-ranging testimony to the encounter with divine being is no mere superstition but a clue that there is such a reality to be experienced.

Christianity's distinctive features gradually became more apparent and illuminating to Lewis. What stood out for Lewis is that in Christianity, the belief in the Incarnation and the narrative of Jesus Christ's life are not advanced as once-upon-a-time stories but as credible history. Christianity is based on oral and written testimony about a particularized figure: it recalls the story of the birth, life, death, burial, Resurrection, and Ascension of Jesus Christ. The historical testimony behind Christianity is exceptional and without parallel in world religions. And today Christianity is constituted by a community of believers who testify in their lives to an experience of the Risen Christ.

In 1929, Lewis finally admitted that "God is God." In 1931, he and Warren left on a motorcycle to visit Whipsnade Zoo. He confessed later that over the thirty-mile trip, he had mysteriously come to believe that Jesus was the Son of God.

After his conversion Lewis would at times still describe Christianity as a myth, though as a myth that turns out to be a fact:

> The heart of Christianity is a myth which is also a fact. The old myth of the Dying God, *without ceasing to be myth* comes down from the heaven of legend and imagination to the earth of history. It *happens*—at a particular date, in a particular place, followed by definable historical consequences. We pass from a Balder or an Osiris, dying nobody knows when or where, to a historical Person crucified . . . *under Pontius Pilate.* By becoming fact it does not cease to be myth: that is the miracle. (C. S. Lewis, *God in the Dock*, pp. 66–67)

Lewis came to see Christianity as living faith, anchored in history, with the power to speak to us concretely about good and evil, fulfillment and failure, life and death.

While Lewis's conversion had a strong intellectual component, it was not mere academic speculation. In Lewis's experience, God gradually becomes more of a vivid, inescapable reality. In a letter to a friend near the time of his conversion, Lewis actually expressed great reluctance about his becoming a convert to Christianity:

> Terrible things are happening to me. The "Spirit" or "Real I" is showing an alarming tendency to become much more personal and is taking the offensive, and behaving just like God. You'd better come on Monday at the latest or I may have entered a monastery. (W. H. Lewis, ed., *Letters*, p. 141)

Lewis did not enter a monastery on that Monday, but very soon afterward he entered the Christian faith. In his own words, he was "brought in kicking, struggling, resentful, and darting his eyes in every direction for a chance of escape" (C. S. Lewis, *Surprised by Joy*, p. 229). God carried him into a relationship with God.

The Feeling Intellect

In his everyday living and in his work as a professor and scholar, Lewis celebrated the fullness of life in God. This newly found faith animated his appreciation of the great goods of creation and motivated his effort to expose the ways in which persons suppress these goods, avoid God, and injure one another:

> Ordinary men have not been so much in love with life as is usually supposed: small as their share of it is, they have found it too much to bear without reducing a large portion of it as nearly to non-life as they can: we love drugs, sleep, irresponsibility, amusement, are more than half in love with easeful death. (W. H. Lewis, *Letters*, p. 190)

In his stories, lectures, poems, and letters, Lewis offered a rich picture of the allure of the Christian faith. He sought to integrate feeling and intellect in a living faith. Whether Lewis's project was to praise some good of creation or to oppose some lifestyle, institution, or philosophy that he judged to be cruel and life-denying, he sought to do so with both intelligence and emotion. Lewis disallowed a radical dualism that places passion on one side and reason on the other. His close friend Austin Farrer observed Lewis's failure to isolate thoughts from feelings:

> No doubt many intellectuals keep a life of feeling somewhere apart, where it will not infect the aseptic purity of their thoughts. If it is a crime to think about all you strongly feel and feel the realities about which you think, then the crime was certainly his. (Como, ed., *C. S. Lewis at the Breakfast Table*, p. 243)

One of the faculties Lewis employed to hone the relation between feeling and intellect in his own life and work was imagination. Fortunately this imagination spilled over into almost all his literary work. His writings—both popular and scholarly—are packed with colorful thought experiments. Readers are asked to rearrange their priorities, to see life from radically different points of view, and to entertain great truths in shifting, sometimes highly fanciful settings. His major fiction, including *The Chronicles of Narnia* and *The Screwtape Letters* and novels such as *Perelandra, That Hideous Strength, The Great Divorce,* and *Till We Have Faces,* represent Lewis's imaginative invention of alternative worlds in which Christianity is explored both intellectually and emotionally. He wanted to capitalize on the mythic dynamism of Christianity, to see its truths in different climates and geographies, even in different worlds.

For Lewis, God was no absentminded administrator or manipulative statesman but a rich, governing, creative reality which, unfettered, evokes great passion, imagination, and love. Lewis would have fully embraced Saint Thomas Aquinas's dictum, "Grace does not destroy nature but perfects it."

Lewis was a catholic Christian devoted to the historic teaching of the church and its creeds, and he did so as a member of the Anglican Communion. He did not preoccupy himself with debating church policy or with settling differences between Christian communities. Instead he prized the unity among Christians, and he always applauded "mere Christianity" rather than a specific tradition within Christianity. He was chiefly interested in reaching those who were alienated from Christianity, those who were skeptical, atheistic, or agnostic, or those who were Christian and yet cut off from the counsel and wisdom of Christian faith.

Lewis was not a political man, though he always stood up for justice and compassion and was not afraid to enter fierce public debate on their behalf. If he had a political enemy, it would be the modern tendency to hunger after power for its own sake, and often at the profound expense of the most vulnerable. Such a lust for pure power is an example of how human desires can be or can become contorted. The desire to exercise physical, emotional, and intellectual abilities is good; the desire to do so while crushing or overshadowing the rights of others is a grave evil.

Lewis relished a self-giving intimacy and the beauty of a truly humane life with its personal relations; he disdained mechanized governments, impersonal public spaces, and artificial mass-produced entertainment. He believed that, at its best, Christianity can speak authentically to who we truly are and can call us to a respectful, even festive, fulfillment. The dimension of fun should not be overshadowed or minimized. Lewis thought of play, humor, and wit as all of a piece in the abundant life to be found in God. This celebration of play and life is what lay behind his more polemical work against political and social forces that threaten to undo us.

Lewis felt driven by a lively sense of the reality and character of God, and his key goal was to be sensitive to this divine presence and its working in him. In commenting on a friend's ability to deny himself so as to allow God more and more of a role in his life, Lewis wrote that nothing makes someone so visible as the desire to be invisible so that something fairer may shine through.

Temperamentally, Lewis was a tangible, feet-on-the-ground man, with a distinctive and colorful personality; he was also someone who sought to be transparent, someone given over to a light and life that stretched out way beyond the limits of his life.

Lewis's adult professional life was spent largely as a scholar-teacher. His lectures were widely known for their depth, humanity, and wit. Despite his scholarly publications and numerous prizes, the deep respect he received from his students, and the popularity of his lectures, an influential group of faculty at Oxford blocked Lewis's professional advancement. They distrusted his Christianity and denigrated his popular writings, especially the children's fiction.

After thirty years at Oxford, Lewis accepted a professorship at Magdalene College, Cambridge. One observer of his inaugural lecture at Cambridge described the lecture as

> brilliant, intellectually exciting, unexpected, and funny as hell—as you can imagine. The hall was crowded, and there were so many capped and gowned dons in the front rows that they looked like a rookery. (Walter Hooper, *C. S. Lewis: A Companion and Guide*, pp. 72–73)

Grief and Joy

Lewis was a bachelor until the 1950s, when he met Helen Joy Davidman, a Jewish poet and writer, and a recent convert to Christianity. They corresponded for some years, and she credits her conversion to having read Lewis's writings. They were legally married in 1956, and after 1957 they lived together at the Kilns, sharing the household with Jack's brother, Warren, until Joy's death from cancer in 1960.

In marrying Joy and becoming a stepfather to her two sons, Douglas and David, Lewis entered an intense period in his life. In March 1957, he wrote to a friend:

> I think I haven't yet told my news. I have lately married a lady who is very ill and probably dying; I shall be left with two stepsons. Thus, as you may guess, great beauty and great tragedy have come into my life. We need your prayers more than ever. . . . (W. H. Lewis, ed., *Letters*, p. 275)

Lewis described his feelings about being a stepfather in a letter to Sister Madeleva, CSC:

Add your prayer for help and guidance in the difficult responsibility of bringing up two orphan stepsons. I have only one qualification if it is one; these two boys are now facing the very same calamity that befell my brother and myself at about the same age. (W. H. Lewis, ed., *Letters*, p. 276)

Lewis's reaction to Joy's death is retold in *A Grief Observed*, which was published by Lewis under the pseudonym N. W. Clerk. The story of their falling in love, the events surrounding their marriage, and the wrenching story of her dying are told in a play, *Shadowlands*, by William Nicholson, which over time became a theatrical production, a British Broadcasting Corporation (BBC) production, and finally a movie.

After Joy's death Lewis wrote:

One thing, however, marriage has done for me. I can never again believe that religion is manufactured out of our unconscious, starved desires and is a substitute for sex. For those few years H. and I feasted on love; every mode of it—solemn and merry, romantic and realistic, sometimes as dramatic as a thunderstorm, sometimes as comfortable and unemphatic as putting on your soft slippers. No cranny of heart or body remained unsatisfied. If God were a substitute for love we ought to have lost all interest in Him. Who'd bother about substitutes when he has the thing itself? But that isn't what happens. We both knew we wanted something besides one another—quite a different kind of something, a quite different kind of want. (C. S. Lewis, *A Grief Observed*, p. 10)

Another of the conclusions that Lewis drew from the experience of marriage was the vulnerability of love. In loving Joy he had opened himself to joy as well as to pain. The very nature of love made any other alternative impossible:

To love at all is to be vulnerable. Love anything, and your heart will certainly be wrung and possibly be broken. If you want to make sure of keeping it intact, you must give your heart to no one, not even to an animal. Wrap it carefully round with hobbies and little luxuries; avoid all entanglements; lock it up safe in the casket or coffin of your selfishness. But in that casket—safe, dark, motionless, air-less—it will change. It will not be broken; it will become unbreakable, impenetrable, irredeemable. (C. S. Lewis, *The Four Loves*, p. 169)

Having loved his wife, Joy, meant he would grieve, and grieve terribly, at her death.

The End of This Life

Lewis died on 22 November 1963, at Oxford, England. It coincided with the deaths of John F. Kennedy and Aldous Huxley, a prominent British essayist, novelist, and mystic. Lewis was a thoroughgoing supernaturalist, deeply committed to the belief in the afterlife of persons because of his understanding of the Incarnation and the Resurrection of Jesus Christ. He did not think of death as oblivion or as an occasion for rebirth in a cyclical pattern of reincarnations. Rather, he thought that death was an awful transition—a hideous, ugly end—the break between soul and body. But he also believed that death was the crossing of a frontier, a doorway to the continuation of an abundant life with God beyond this life as we know it. In the end, humans are saved not because they desire God but because God lovingly desires them and enables them to participate in eternal life.

Lewis's Belief in the Incarnation

Central to Lewis's spirituality is the mystery of the Incarnation of the Divine Word in Christ Jesus, a mystery that redeems humankind. For Lewis, the very heart of Christianity is a miracle:

The Christian story is precisely the story of one grand miracle, the Christian assertion being that what is beyond all space and time, what is uncreated, eternal, came into nature, into human nature, descended into His own universe, and rose again, bringing nature up with Him. It is precisely one great miracle. (C. S. Lewis, *God in the Dock*, p. 80)

The miracle of the Eternal Word's descent and Incarnation and Christ's humanity rising from the dead and ascending is not a mere display of divine power. It is the mystery of God's love redeeming us.

Human wickedness alienates us from God, estranges us from one another, and leaves us, as it were, chained prisoners of evil. Humankind is hemmed in by our own petty sins and by greater shared evils—whether these forces are internal to us or external. By entering this world, assuming and sharing human nature, embracing sorrow, and demonstrating God's love, Christ ransomed humanity from the imprisoning powers of sin and death and gained release and freedom. Faith in Christ's Resurrection is faith in God's action to provide for each person a way to be delivered from evil, to be liberated from life-denying forces, habits, works, and institutions. The Incarnation and self-offering of Christ open a door for us to begin a new life, correcting and fulfilling our natural relations and initiating a deeper, supernatural life. A relationship with Christ plants the seed of eternal life.

Themes of Lewis's Spirituality

Lewis's spirituality yields many themes for fruitful meditation. Here are four key currents that inform the fifteen meditations that follow.

Desire and Longing

For Lewis, the heart of the spiritual life is to fully appreciate that we are creatures, not the Creator, and to discover the many ways in which our desire for various created goods can be caught up in an all-embracing relationship with the Creator and Author of nature. Longing for different goods should not be shunned but integrated and understood in the expanded terrain that God has authored for our individual and mutual fulfillment.

The Feeling Intellect

Lewis's work calls us to personal integrity, both emotional and intellectual. If Lewis is right, then Christian faith invites and even requires an integration of feeling and intellect. Some forms of Christianity seem to divorce the two, leaving the believer on the verge of being irritated that he or she even has an inquiring mind or an affectionate heart. Lewis, on the other hand, celebrates the role of mind and heart, and their integrated relationship in personal living and acting.

The Natural and the Supernatural

Lewis held that the adoration of the God who made nature enables us to experience and live in nature with respect, wonder, and intelligence. Just as Lewis pressed for an integration of feeling and intellect, he fought for an integrated understanding of the natural and the supernatural.

Imagination

Lewis offers us different ways in which to cultivate a life of imagination that further our engagement in this world and our exploration of community life. The development of an individual's and a community's imagination can play a central role in cultivating a rich relationship with God.

Lewis for Today

These four themes, or motifs, are themselves interwoven. It is because of the Incarnation and the miraculous redemption through Christ that our imagination is challenged and kindled, and we are able to see a profound integration of the natural and the supernatural, feeling and intellect, and the end of our deepest longing: a full life lived before the fullness of a loving God.

Lewis's work is especially important today. In our culture spirituality is often marketed along slick lines, in accord with strict fundamentalism or in the name of some generic, vague feelings about a higher power or a hope in something more. Lewis banishes the temptation to think that classical Christianity is somehow dull, intellectually otiose, or rendered useless due to contemporary experience. In Lewis one finds a critically reflective, vibrant voice that compels us to question the often unchallenged skepticism and overconfident fundamentalism of our age. And Lewis is important for another reason: for relaying the joy that he believes awaits us with God, "The whole man is to drink joy from the fountain of joy" (C. S. Lewis, *The Weight of Glory*, p. 14).

✧ Meditation 1 ✧

Awakened Desire

Theme: Our desires and longing can provide clues about the God who creates and loves us.

Opening prayer: Come, Holy Spirit, fill our hearts. Kindle in us the fire of your love.

About Lewis

As a youth, Lewis caught what he would later describe as a glimpse of something profoundly fulfilling, something more spacious and full than this world. Lewis describes one such experience: "I was uplifted into huge regions of northern sky, I desired with almost sickening intensity something never to be described" (*Surprised by Joy*, p. 17).

For a time in his adolescence and early adulthood, Lewis dismissed this haunting sense of the reality of a higher, enlarged world. He tossed off any religious significance to these experiences and shed the Christianity of his upbringing. During that period Lewis wrote:

> I believe in no religion. There is absolutely no proof for any of them, and from a philosophical standpoint Christianity is not even the best. All religions, that is, all mythologies to give them their proper name are merely

man's own invention. (Walter Hooper, *Through Joy and Beyond*, p. 57)

But later on, as he came to maturity, Lewis became transfixed once again by this longing for contact and union with a reality greater than his own, a reality that seemed to be hinted at in both religious and nonreligious settings. This longing had a potency, depth, and character that was not easy to explain away as disordered adolescent emotions or to place in a box labeled "idle superstitions."

By his early thirties, Lewis could no longer think of the human longing for—and the reported experience of—a greater divine reality as mere childhood invention. In part, he was impressed by the widespread witness across many cultures and many eras of this longing for a joy beyond this world and the sense that something beyond this world, a divine reality, was calling us to itself:

> What is universal is not the particular picture, but the arrival of some message, not perfectly intelligible, which wakes this desire and sets men longing for something East or West of the world; something possessed, if at all, only in the act of desiring it, and lost so quickly that the craving itself becomes craved; something that tends inevitably to be confused with common or even with vile satisfactions lying close to hand, yet which is able, if any man faithfully live through the dialectic of its successive births and deaths, to lead him at last where true joys are to be found. (C. S. Lewis, *The Pilgrim's Regress*, pp. 156–157)

Through his own study of religious experience and the arguments for and against a belief in God, Lewis came to think of the longing for joy as something that echoes and reflects the reality of God. By his lights, the search for a joy that is wider than this world is bound up with a search for the God who made us and all worlds.

Lewis's early and mature longing for a fulfillment in God did not consist in repudiating the pleasures of this world. He sought instead to uncover the source and richer meaning of the goods of creation. The pleasures he experienced and his desire for richer fulfillment signaled for Lewis not the birth of egomania and disordered demands but the awakening of an appreciation that this world of genuine goods points to a deeper and higher good. It is as though Lewis began by being fascinated by the brilliant color and texture of an expansive cloth laid out before him and then gradually realized that it might also make up a flag of a great country. It was this richer country that included this world but also went beyond it that Lewis would spend his mature life exploring.

Pause: What do you yearn for?

Lewis's Words

The settled happiness and security which we all desire, God withholds from us by the very nature of the world: but joy, pleasure, and merriment He has scattered broadcast. We are never safe, but we have plenty of fun, and some ecstasy. It is not hard to see why. The security we crave would teach us to rest our hearts in this world and oppose an obstacle to our return to God: a few moments of happy love, a landscape, a symphony, a merry meeting with our friends, a bath or a football match, have no such tendency. Our Father refreshes us on the journey with some pleasant inns, but will not encourage us to mistake them for home. (C. S. Lewis, *The Problem of Pain,* p. 115)

Reflection

Philosophy begins in wonder, according to the ancient philosopher Aristotle. As such, philosophy begins with something like the curiosity, interests, and awakened desire of a child. Lewis thought that this sense of wonder was not something that we should restrict for childhood or for only the odd, exotic occurrence: the grandeur of a mountain or a startling view of another planet. For Lewis, the bare fact of our existence in this world counts as something worthy of wonder and fascination. As Lewis says, "No man would find an abiding strangeness on the Moon unless he were the sort of man who would find it in his own back garden" (*On Stories and Other Essays on Literature*, p. 12).

First and foremost, Lewis stood for taking this "back garden" wonder seriously. The very existence of life is something to find astounding!

We often take so many things for granted, not the least of which is our very existence. A little thought can cure us of this. We can imagine that the world could have existed without us, indeed without any of those we know. Taken to the extreme, we can even imagine that the earth had not existed, but that instead different worlds were in its place. We often are aware of this contingency but fail to take it seriously. In cultivating an imaginative appreciation of the radical contingency of the cosmos, one can recover some of the wonder we may have felt as children. Just as Lewis tries to evoke wonder about our very existence, he invites us to give imagination free play so that we may increase our sense of wonder about the nature of the reality behind and pervading this contingent cosmos—God.

In imaginatively engaging a picture of the God of Christianity, we encounter a God who did not have to create a cosmos. The picture, rather, is of a being of outpouring love and goodness, who made a cosmos for the sake of love. This God is One who can be encountered through the goods of creation, its riches and its opportunities.

The kind of Christian spirituality that drew Lewis in and the kind that he came to defend involve a central, enthralling, life-affirming love of creation. Out of love for the goods of creation came an awakened desire for the God of creation. Conversely, out of a love and worship of the God of creation came a more refined and exuberant love for the goods of this world.

✧ In *Letters to Malcolm*, Lewis writes:

You first taught me the great principle "Begin where you are." I had thought one had to start by summoning up what we believe about the goodness and greatness of God. . . . You turned to the brook and once more splashed your burning face and hands in the little water-fall and said, "Why not begin with this?" (P. 88)

Find the place to begin your prayer and begin. Let God manifest the glory in creation.

✧ Bring your desires before God. In your journal or on a sheet of paper, finish the sentences: I long for . . . I desire . . . I want . . . Repeat the exercise a second time. Bring the most significant desires up from your heart, and offer them to the God who hears you. Talk with God about how these desires are invitations into relationship.

✧ Many people can recall an experience of their childhood or adolescent years in which they were manifestly aware of God's presence, with a quality different than ordinary. If this is true for you, take some time to remember this experience: Where were you? What happened? How were you affected? Thank God now for the manifestation of this presence, this theophany.

✧ As you plan to enjoy some activity—a happy encounter with a friend, an hour of exercise, a meal, or a romp with your dog or cat—imagine God's taking pleasure in your enjoyment. Ask the God of life to be with you in this pleasant event, enjoying creation in you and through you and with you.

✧ Go for a long walk or bicycle ride, saying to yourself as you move, breathe, and take in your surroundings, "The Spirit of God fills the whole world." Bring back something that will remind you of the glories of creation.

God's Word

You, Yahweh, are all I have,
and you give me all I need: my life is in your hands.
How wonderful are your gifts to me;
how good they are!

I praise Yahweh, who guides me,
and in the night my conscience teaches me.
I am always aware of your presence;
you are near, and nothing can shake me.
And so I am full of happiness and joy,
and I always feel secure.
Because you will not allow me
to go to the world of the dead;
you will not abandon to the depths below
the one you love.
You will show me the path that leads to life;
your presence fills me with joy,
and your help brings pleasure forever.

(Psalm 16:5–11)

Closing prayer: Send forth your Spirit and we will be re-created, and you will renew the face of the earth.

A Divine Imagination

Theme: Imagination is a fruitful instrument of grace.

Opening prayer: O Holy God of Life, so fill our imagination that we may find ourselves ever more fully in your presence.

About Lewis

Lewis's evaluation of the world was tested on the battlefields of World War I. Being in the frontline trenches, as he was in 1918, to receive the final German attack on the Western Front, left traces that can be like poison in the life of a survivor. During the war Lewis wrote that God seemed to be a distant phantom that some called the Good. After lengthy and profound meditation, Lewis came to wonder whether the human appetite for war, with its acts of cruelty and hatred, happens because humans are the phantoms, not God.

Lewis's inquiry into whether God exists involved the use of imagination—the ability to picture different ways in which reality may be structured. Reflecting on his own life and human history involved a study of facts, but at a certain point, it also involved imaginatively looking at these facts from different angles. Lewis unleashed the childlike and probing question, "Why?" Why is there good and evil? Why does the cosmos exist? World War I occurred, but did it have to occur? His imagination allowed him to see things very differently, to construct alternative larger frameworks to interpret the moral goods and evils of humanity, to imaginatively wonder whether there is or is not a God.

According to Lewis, it is in virtue of our God-oriented imagination that we often find ourselves at odds with suffering and death. We quite easily can imagine a playing field of significance larger than "the facts of natural history." Imagination enables us to question the stubborn assumptions of our culture and the prevailing picture of the limits of the world.

For Lewis, it was on the basis of imaginative reflection on the contingent nature of the world that he was drawn to acknowledge a being that is noncontingent and sheer goodness. He was moved to conversion, in part, through G. K. Chesterton's proposal that Christianity does justice to the peculiar tension we feel of being both at home in the world and yet restless and unsatisfied. Chesterton's lively treatment of Christianity in *The Everlasting Man* profoundly opened Lewis's mind and heart to the tension or dialectic in which humans find themselves to be situated.

Chesterton encouraged Lewis to trust his natural revolt against evil and his relish for all that is good, and to question what this tension between evil and good tells about the human condition and the need for God. Lewis's imaginative investigation of Christian faith grew in stages, from his reflections while convalescing in a hospital in France in 1918 to his conversion in Oxford, England, in the 1930s. His own imaginative activity throughout these years usually involved facts, questions, new interpretations, and often humor.

Pause: Ask yourself, How has my imagination helped me in solving life's problems?

Lewis's Words

Lewis attempted to explain his position on the composite unity of each human being, and on the inner quarreling and rebellion that attends our present condition:

Almost the whole of Christian theology could perhaps be deduced from the two facts (a) That men make coarse jokes, and (b) That they feel the dead to be uncanny. The coarse joke proclaims that we have here an animal which finds its own animality either objectionable or funny. Unless there had been a quarrel between the spirit and the organism I do not see how this could be: it the very mark of the two not being "at home" together. But it is very difficult to imagine such a state of affairs as original—to suppose a creature which from the very first was half shocked and half tickled to death at the mere fact of being the creature it is. I do not perceive that dogs see anything funny about being dogs: I suspect that angels see nothing funny about being angels. Our feeling about the dead is equally odd. It is idle to say that we dislike corpses because we are afraid of ghosts. You might say with equal truth that we fear ghosts because we dislike corpses—for the ghost owes much of its horror to the associated ideas of pallor, decay, coffins, shrouds, and worms. In reality we hate the division which makes possible the conception of either corpse or ghost. Because the thing ought not to be divided, each of the halves into which it falls by division is detestable. . . . Once accept the Christian doctrine that man was originally a unity and that the present division is unnatural, and all the phenomena fall into place. . . .

I ought, perhaps to point out that the argument is not in the least affected by the value-judgments we make about ghost stories or coarse humour. You may hold that both are bad. You may hold that both, though they result (like clothes) from the Fall, are (like clothes) the proper way to deal with the Fall once it has occurred: that while perfected and recreated Man will no longer experience that kind of laughter or that kind of shudder, yet here and now not to feel the horror and not to see the joke is to be less than human. But either way the facts bear witness to our present maladjustment. (C. S. Lewis, *Miracles*, pp. 132–133)

Reflection

A disciplined, active imagination is needed in order to pull together the different stages of our life and the various currents at work within us. As Lewis suggests, jokes and imagination can reveal quite a lot about one's understanding and sensibility. Typically, jesting and imagining require a certain elasticity, an ability to see things in different lights.

If Lewis is right, the imagination may aid us in catching a glimpse not just of how things are but of how things should be. Sin involves a fracture between the self and God, the self and nature, the self from itself, and the self from others. Imagination can help us see that our world and we ourselves are indeed severed and splintered, and that our rebellion against this broken condition is important. Sometimes this is revealed not so much in our most solemn moments as it is at times when we imaginatively jest about our predicament and the absurdity of our misguided seriousness and narrow obsessions that can govern our life.

A playful, life-affirming humor and imagination can help us combat the despair that would have us all conclude that there is no alternative to a fractured existence. Lewis did not pin his whole conversion on imagination, humor, and the longing for God. But they all had a role in shaping his character and opening him up to the possibility of a powerful redemptive life in relation to God.

✧ What are your favorite jokes, farces, comedies? Use a page in your journal to reflect on why you like them, and what they may tell you about yourself and the world.

✧ Think of a change that would be a benefit to your life. Imagine the scene with yourself behaving the way you desire to behave and others responding in a way that you hope and ardently wish for. Imagine the change has already occurred as you ask for God's guidance, wise empowerment, and blessing.

✧ Place yourself in the quiet presence of God. Ask for the grace and talent you need in one area of creative endeavor, such as songwriting, singing, playing an instrument, drawing, painting, sculpting, dancing, playwriting, producing, inventing, crafting. Write on a piece of paper the talent you most desire. Compose a prayer in which you ask God for this gift. Compose another prayer in which you thank God for receiving this gift. Pray the first prayer every morning for a week. Pray the second prayer every evening for a week.

✧ Prayer may be assisted by imagination in an endless number of ways. A good friend gained enormously by ritually putting her troubles to sleep. She found herself near despair with overwork, and, wracked with insomnia, she lay awake surrounded by huge stacks of paper and books—all of which seemed to cry out for attention. As it happened she was in a room with an unoccupied bed. She piled all the books and paper on the other bed, put a blanket over them as though she were putting someone to bed, turned off the lights, said a brief prayer, and was soon enjoying the best sleep in months. Is there some imaginative ritual you can enact to neutralize your stresses of today?

✧ Read meditatively the following poem, "Eden's Courtesy," by Lewis:

> Such natural love twixt beast and man we find
> That children all desire an animal book,
> And all brutes, not perverted from their kind,
> Woo us with whinny, tongue, tail, song, or look;
>   So much of Eden's courtesy yet remains.
> But when a creature's dread, or mine, has built
> A wall between, I think I feel the pains
> That Adam earned and do confess my guilt.
>   For till I tame sly fox and timorous hare
> And lording lion in myself, no peace
> Can be without; but after, I shall dare
> Uncage the shadowy zoo and war will cease;
>   Because the brutes within, I do not doubt,
> Are archetypal of the brutes without.
>
> (C. S. Lewis, *Poems*, p. 98)

God's Word

May God grant me to speak with judgment
and to have thoughts worthy of what I have received;
for he is the guide even of wisdom
and the corrector of the wise.
. . . .
There is in [wisdom] a spirit that is intelligent, holy,
unique, manifold, subtle,
mobile, clear, unpolluted,
distinct, invulnerable, loving the good, keen,
irresistible, beneficent, humane,
steadfast, sure, free from anxiety,
all-powerful, overseeing all,
and penetrating through all spirits
that are intelligent, pure, and altogether subtle.
For wisdom is more mobile than any motion;
because of her pureness she pervades and penetrates all
        things.
For she is a breath of the power of God,
and a pure emanation of the glory of the Almighty.

                        (Wisdom of Solomon 7:15–25)

Closing prayer: Life-giving God, lead us to use and enjoy the power of imagination. Forgive us when we let this great gift atrophy, or be misused. Send us wisdom to guide our imagination.

A Divine Sensibility

Theme: Conversion and openness to God involves a new sensibility that integrates reason and feelings.

Opening prayer: O wisdom of God, enable us to learn your ways. So bring together our thoughts and feelings that our acts may be filled with your life-giving Spirit.

About Lewis

Lewis's religious conversion was not a solitary happening but an event interwoven with the ways of friendship. Lewis was challenged to come to the Christian faith by the great medieval scholar J. R. R. Tolkien, and by several other friends. For a long time, Lewis had presumed that Christian narratives of a dying and resurrected God-man were too primitive, too drenched in superstition to have any purchase on the modern mind. Through Tolkien, Hugo Dyson, and others, he began to appreciate how Christian belief is built on historical testimony and on an expansive understanding of the cosmos.

Tolkien challenged Lewis to link together both intellect and poetic sensibility. So long as Lewis stuck to his antireligious naturalism with its narrow horizon, he could not fully explain or be reconciled to his poetic longing and desire for fulfillment. In recounting his movement toward conversion, Lewis later wrote:

> The two hemispheres of my mind were in the sharpest contrast. On the one side a many-islanded sea of poetry and myth; on the other a glib and shallow "rationalism." Nearly all that I loved I believed to be imaginary; nearly all that I believed to be real I thought grim and meaningless. The exceptions were certain people (whom I loved and believed to be real) and nature herself. (*Surprised by Joy*, p. 170)

An articulate, intelligent Christianity spoke to both hemispheres: his feelings and his reason. Through friendship, reflection, and personal prayer, what took shape was a fresh, unified, and open Christian sensibility.

Lewis's coming to a major change in his life was not a matter of just learning a new fact but of truly being altered by what he took to be the facts, "What you see and hear depends a good deal on where you are standing: it also depends on what sort of person you are" (C. S. Lewis, *The Magician's Nephew*, p. 123). Conversion involved a profound shift both in terms of viewpoint and viewer. To see the world as God's creation called for Lewis to develop a new sensibility, just as a sailor acquires sea legs as the boat leaves harbor in order to achieve balance on the ship and have a steady gaze at the sea.

What Lewis reported was that his conversion had set up a vivid process all its own. The movement developed a dynamic and a pace taking him from a secular, closed world to a new identity in Christ. Lewis came to believe and to see that he was subject to a reality that is far more fully and profoundly alive than he had dreamed.

Pause: Ask yourself: Have I ever had the experience of being found by God? Was I terrified? Was I overjoyed?

Lewis's Words

> It is always shocking to meet life where we thought we were alone. "Look out!" we cry, "it's *alive*." And therefore

this is the very point at which so many draw back—I would have done so myself if I could—and proceed no further with Christianity. An "impersonal God"—well and good. A subjective God of beauty, truth and goodness, inside our own heads—better still. A formless life-force surging through us, a vast power which we can tap—best of all. But God Himself, alive, pulling at the other end of the cord, perhaps approaching at an infinite speed, the hunter, king, husband—that is quite another matter. There comes a moment when the children who have been playing at burglars hush suddenly: was that a *real* footstep in the hall? There comes a moment when people who have been dabbling in religion ("Man's search for God"!) suddenly draw back. Supposing we really found Him? We never meant it to come to *that!* Worse still, supposing He had found us? (C. S. Lewis, *Miracles*, pp. 96–97)

No man was, I suppose, ever so mad as to think that man, or all creation, *filled* the Divine Mind; if we are a small thing to space and time, space and time are a much smaller thing to God. It is a profound mistake to imagine that Christianity ever intended to dissipate the bewilderment and even the terror, the sense of our own nothingness, which come upon us when we think about the nature of things. It comes to intensify them. Without such sensations there is no religion. Many a man, brought up in the glib profession of some shallow form of Christianity, who comes through reading Astronomy to realise for the first time how majestically indifferent most reality is to man, and who perhaps abandons his religion on that account, may at that moment be having his first genuinely religious experience.

Christianity does not involve the belief that all things were made for man. It does involve the belief that God loves man and for his sake became man and died. (C. S. Lewis, *Miracles*, pp. 52–53)

Reflection

In Lewis's view, Christianity is not some narrowing down of the human spirit but its opening and flourishing in a harmonious balance. In God our life becomes animated by an abounding, gracious presence. As Origen of Alexandria put it, "by participation [in the Word] we are raised from deadness and enlightened." With this enlightenment comes powers of discrimination and imagination, and an influx of greater depth and vitality. Our experience of nature involves the influx of sensations that require focus and simplified attention in order to engage and transform us. Similarly, our experience of nature as God's gift involves an openness to an influx of sensations. Lewis would subscribe to the following lesson:

> An adult must learn to be yielding and careless like a child if he were to enjoy nature polymorphously. He needs to slip into old clothes so that he could feel free to stretch out on the hay beside the brook and bathe in a meld of physical sensations: the smell of hay and of horse dung; the warmth of the ground, its hard and soft contours; the warmth of the sun tempered by breeze; the tickling of an ant making its way up the calf of his leg; the play of shifting leaf shadows on his face; the sound of water over the pebbles and boulders, the sound of cicadas and distant traffic. Such an environment might break all the formal rules of euphony and aesthetics, substituting confusion for order, and yet be wholly satisfying. (Yi-Fu Tuan, *Topophilia*, p. 96)

✧ Go to your backyard or to a nearby park. For fifteen minutes just look and listen. If something catches your eye or attracts you by its sound, attend to it with concentration. Find the beauty in it. At the end of your stay, recite three times to yourself, "Glory to God in the highest, and peace to God's people on earth."

✧ Lewis found terror an honest emotion. When have you been frightened or terrified? Did you pray?

✧ Mountains, oceans, desert spaces, and night skies speak of the grandeur and vastness of nature and of the Creator. What natural environments speak to you of your relation to God?

✧ The things of nature can increase and refine our sensibility in various ways:
✦ focusing on an object, such as a leaf, a flower, a singular tree
✦ viewing a panoramic setting or regarding the landscape from a fixed position
✦ immersing all one's senses while engaging in an activity, such as swimming, mountain climbing, birding
Which of these is already a part of your spiritual life? Which would be good for you to engage in today?

✧ Lewis had a zest for hiking with friends, especially when tea was served at the end of it. A good hike cultivates a certain sensibility—a pace, a blend between attention and

physical exertion, conversation, humor, and silence. Go on a hike with friends with the desire to increase your attentiveness to all things—to various and sundry things, to your own ability and agility. At the end, thank God for the joy this hike gave you.

God's Word

Wisdom is radiant and unfading,
and she is easily discerned by those who love her,
and is found by those who seek her.
She hastens to make herself known to those who desire
        her.
One who rises early to seek her will have no difficulty,
for she will be found sitting at the gate.
To fix one's thought on her is perfect understanding,
and one who is vigilant on her account will soon be free
        from care,
because she goes about seeking those worthy of her,
and she graciously appears to them in their paths,
and meets them in every thought.
                            (Wisdom of Solomon 6:12–16)

Closing prayer: O God, may we not flee from your coming and at your appearance in our life. May we become more sensitive to your presence and to your glory in creation.

✧ **Meditation 4** ✧

Prayer and Reality

Theme: Prayer is a vital bond between us and our Creator.

Opening prayer: Teach us to pray, O holy and lifegiving God.

About Lewis

The first prayer that Lewis recorded as an adult was the bare acknowledgment of the existence of God. He later came to pray in more explicit terms, invoking the God revealed in Jesus Christ. What marked the recorded prayers was Lewis's realization that he was addressing a living reality, a timeless being of supreme knowledge, goodness, and power. The difficulty for most pray-ers, including Lewis himself, is due to the fact that in this relationship the personal contact of prayer is "between embryonic, incomplete persons (ourselves) and the utterly concrete Person" (C. S. Lewis, *The World's Last Night*, p. 8).

Few of Lewis's own prayers are in print, but he thought it important to speak about prayer in a public way. In 1941, during the Second World War, he addressed the Royal Air Force in Abingdon, England. These addresses to the RAF were broadcast over the BBC, making C. S. Lewis's voice the second most recognized voice in England at that time, after Winston Churchill's.

Even though Lewis's prose was measured and rational, listeners could readily discern that his words were profound ones emerging from his intellect and his feelings:

> The effect he made is hard to describe a generation later, and I doubt whether even a contemporary diary could quite convey it. He never showed any emotion, although I think his listeners knew instinctively that his thoughts had been hammered out in the furnace rather than stored inside a glacier. (Como, ed., *C. S. Lewis at the Breakfast Table*, p. 188)

A sequence can be found in the recommendations Lewis gave about praying. The soul is to gather itself together, recollect itself, then acknowledge its Creator, and finally move ever more closely and profoundly into the life of God. "Confession and penance are its threshold, adoration its sanctuary, the presence and vision and enjoyment of God its bread and wine" (C. S. Lewis, *The World's Last Night*, p. 8).

Lewis addresses the issue of what happens when we find we cannot pray in this way:

> I've just found in an old note-book a poem, with no author's name attached, which is rather relevant to something we were talking about a few weeks ago—I mean, the haunting fear that there is no-one listening, and that what we call prayer is soliloquy: someone talking to himself. . . . Here is the poem.
>
>> They tell me, Lord, that when I seem
>> To be in speech with you,
>> Since but one voice is heard, it's all a dream,
>> One talker aping two.
>> Sometimes it is, yet not as they
>> Conceive it. Rather, I
>> Seek in myself the things I hoped to say,
>> But lo!, my wells are dry.
>> Then, seeing me empty, you forsake
>> The listener's role and through

My dumb lips breathe and into utterance wake
The thoughts I never knew.
And thus you neither need reply
Nor can; thus, while we seem
Two talkers, thou art One forever, and I
No dreamer, but thy dream.
(C. S. Lewis, *Letters to Malcolm*, pp. 67–68)

In all his talks and writings about prayer, Lewis highlighted the connection between the most rudimentary elements of spirituality and the mystery of the presence of God in and through creation. Simple prayer sets us on a trail that leads ever deeper into communion with God.

Pause: Ask yourself, What are my greatest fears about prayer?

Lewis's Words

An ordinary simple Christian kneels down to say his prayers. He is trying to get into touch with God. But if he is a Christian he knows that what is prompting him to pray is also God: God, so to speak, inside him. But he also knows that all his real knowledge of God comes through Christ, the Man who was God—that Christ is standing beside him, helping him to pray, praying for him. You see what is happening. God is the thing to which he is praying—the goal he is trying to reach. God is also the thing inside him which is pushing him on—the motive power. God is also the road or bridge along which he is being pushed to that goal. So that the whole threefold life of the three-personal Being is actually going on in that ordinary little bedroom where an ordinary man is saying his prayers. (C. S. Lewis, *Mere Christianity*, p. 127)

Reflection

Lewis counseled that we should trust in a God who hears prayer, but at the same time we should not lose our sense of the astonishment and wonder of prayer:

> The possibility of personal intercourse between the little, hairless bipeds called Men and the inconceivable, self-existent Being which underlies all phenomena and all space and time, may seem to such people nothing surprising, nothing that we had not a right to expect. If the fact that it appears outrageous to those who have had a purely scientific upbringing startles any such Christian into the realization that, in a sense, it really is outrageous, not to be thought of without amazement and trembling, then it will have done him good. (Hooper, *C. S. Lewis: A Companion and Guide*, pp. 379–380)

Yet God's omnipotence, omniscience, omnipresence, goodness, and love are the foundation for hope and trust, engendered and nurtured in prayer.

Upon conversion we not only receive the gift of faith but we also find a new reference point, a ground and a horizon for ourselves. If the eternal God is all knowing, then God knows who we are: our past, our present, and whatever can be known of the future. The omnipresence of God secures the viability of prayer at all times and in all places. The omnipotence of God enables God to concur in our prayers of petition and to receive our praise and thanksgiving at any time and in any place.

For Lewis, prayer and meditation constitute the great point where we can encounter the God of life and ourselves insofar as we become more truly alive. Prayer can hallow or bless our life, just as our life can, in a sense, inform and ratify our prayers.

✧ Reread the previous "Lewis's Words" section. Reflect on the threefold way in which God is present in your prayer. Compose your own prayers of gratitude to each Person of the Trinity.

✧ Clement of Alexandria writes, "All our life is a festival: being persuaded that God is everywhere present on all sides, we praise him as we till the ground, we sing hymns as we sail the sea, we feel his inspiration in all that we do" (John Oulton and Henry Chadwick, comps., *Alexandrian Christianity*, vol. 2, p. 115). As you begin each activity today, invite God's inspiration. Aloud or silently, sing a favorite hymn of praise.

✧ Reflect on the divine attributes: God's omnipotence, omniscience, supreme goodness, omnipresence. To jar one's earthbound view of God, look at some of the recent photographs taken from outer space in order to inspire your sense of grandeur.

✧ Lewis liked to say his prayers while walking home from the university or riding in trains. Find a simple prayer or a favorite short biblical passage that you can use this week while you are riding or walking between the sites of your daily life.

God's Word

Pray in the Spirit at all times in every prayer and supplication. To that end keep alert and always persevere in supplication for all the saints. (Ephesians 6:18)

Closing prayer: O God, you know us and care for us intimately. May our prayers be a living trust in your loving presence in our life. May our life this day be a prayer for your visitation.

Mindfulness

Theme: Mindful delight in creation is sacred.

Opening prayer: O Creator of the universe, we give you thanks for the pleasures of this life. Teach us to be faithful stewards of these gifts.

About Lewis

Lewis was a medieval and Renaissance scholar. As such he immersed himself in the cosmic worldview of those centuries in which joy and dancing were given center stage. In talking about this worldview, he said:

> I am thinking in particular of one medieval picture which represents the Intelligence of the Primum Mobile itself. It is of course wholly symbolical; they knew perfectly well that such a creature—it had no body—could not be literally depicted at all. But the symbol chosen is delightfully significant. It is a picture of a girl dancing and playing a tambourine; a picture of gaiety, almost of frolic. And why not? These spheres are moved by love, by intellectual desire, never sated because they can never completely assimilate themselves to their object, and never frustrated because they continually do so to the fullest extent which

their nature admits or requires. Their existence is thus one of delight. The motions of the universe are to be conceived not as those of a machine or even an army, but rather as a dance, a festival, a symphony, a ritual, a carnival, or all these in one. They are the unimpeded movement of the most perfect impulse towards the most perfect Object.

A modern mind will of course say that the men of that age fashioned heaven in the likeness of Earth and, because they liked high pomps, the Mass, coronations, pageants, tournaments, carols, attributed such activities *par excellence* to the translunary world. But remember that they thought it was the other way round. (C. S. Lewis, *Studies in Medieval and Renaissance Literature,* p. 60)

This scholarly outlook had repercussions on Lewis's lifestyle. He enjoyed the pleasures of life in a wholehearted way as the gifts of God. He especially loved the great pleasures of life that are found in friendships and in marriage. As well, he loved walks, teas, poetry, meals, humor, intellectual sport, and good wine. He also knew how to practice austerity and to be disciplined in his inner life and his outer behavior.

Lewis held that balance is always in order. Simplicity, care, respect, and restraint are all needed. Lewis was keenly aware of the subtle ways in which selfishness, cruelty, and fear can poison the good of pleasure. Commenting on the ease with which an author can create evil characters in fiction, Lewis writes:

To make a character worse than oneself it is only necessary to release imaginatively from control some of the bad passions which, in real life, are always straining at the leash; the Satan, the Iago, the Becky Sharp, within each of us, is always there and only too ready, the moment the leash is slipped, to come out and have in our books that holiday we try to deny them in our lives. (*A Preface to Paradise Lost,* p. 100)

So Lewis held that we cannot adopt an ethic that says "anything goes"; discipline has its place. He had tasted the difficulties of life in the social dynamics of an all-male boarding school, in the quarreling among the women who lived and worked in the household of Mrs. Moore, and in his brother's addiction to alcohol. In each of these, he recognized the imprisoning quality of pleasures gone astray.

Nevertheless, while believing that vigilance about addictions and healthy moderation must be practiced, Lewis and his friends enjoyed to the full a festive companionship, whether drinking a nice wine, going on a hike, having tea at the end of the day, or fraternally battling one another in vigorous and witty debate. Moderation and discipline can enhance and protect great God-given pleasures.

Pause: How do you understand the relation between pleasure and God? What does it mean that God is a God of wise pleasure?

Lewis's Words

Aren't there bad, unlawful pleasures? Certainly there are. But in calling them "bad pleasures" I take it we are using a kind of shorthand. We mean "pleasures snatched by unlawful acts." It is the stealing of the apple that is bad, not the sweetness. The sweetness is still a beam from the glory. That does not palliate the stealing. It makes it worse. There is sacrilege in the theft. We have abused a holy thing. . . .

I have tried . . . to make every pleasure into a channel of adoration. I don't mean simply by giving thanks for it. One must of course give thanks, but I mean something different. How shall I put it?

We can't—or I can't—hear the song of a bird simply as a sound. Its meaning or message ("That's a bird") comes with it inevitably. . . . This heavenly fruit is instantly redolent of the orchard where it grew. This sweet air whispers of the country from whence it blows. It is a message. We know we are being touched by a finger of that right hand at which there are pleasures for evermore. (C. S. Lewis, *Letters to Malcolm*, pp. 89–90)

Reflection

According to a tradition in philosophy, reasoned, moral living is itself an art. Moral living is not a matter of bare scientific induction, mathematical probability, or logical deduction. Both reasoning and living are guided by wisdom. Some of the terms for referring to the art of moral reasoning and living are practical reason *(phronesis)*, prudence *(prudentia)*, and wisdom *(sophia)*. In Lewis's view, the development of a wise, artful reasoning and living is at the very center of a life of pleasure and joy in and with God.

Vices are to be met, according to Lewis, and defeated by the opposite virtue. Developing virtue can be motivated by discerning an even richer pleasure in reasoned, moral living. Thus, it is for a higher pleasure that the pleasure of food or drink should be enjoyed responsibly and innocently. It is for divine fulfillment that we are bidden to live wisely. This fulfillment is based not simply on expectations for a future life but on a living relationship with God in the present. "Where, except in the present, can the Eternal be met?" (C. S. Lewis, *Christian Reflections,* p. 113).

✧ Bring to mind and heart some of the pleasures in your life, and lift them up to God in thanksgiving.

✧ We are called to be stewards of the gifts of God; this includes gifts of pleasure. For whom do you exercise this excellent stewardship? Spend your prayer time reflecting on this.

✧ Lewis said once of his own wife, Joy, "She liked more things and liked them more than any one I have known" (*A Grief Observed,* p. 18). Can you say this about someone you know? Plan to spend some celebratory time with that person this week.

✧ Meditate on the following passage from Lewis's writings, and write your thoughts and feelings about it:

"Creatures are not born with desires unless satisfaction for those desires exists. . . . If I find in myself a desire which no experience in this world can satisfy, the most probable explanation is that I was made for another world. If none of my earthly pleasures satisfy it, that does not prove that the universe is a fraud. Probably earthly pleasures were never meant to satisfy it, but only to arouse it, to suggest the real thing." (*Mere Christianity*, p. 106)

God's Word

When God established the heavens, I was there,
When God drew a circle on the face of the deep,
made firm the skies above,
established the fountains of the deep,
and assigned to the sea its limit,
so that the waters might not transgress his command,
When God marked out the foundations of the earth,
then I was beside him like a little child,
being daily God's delight
exulting before God always,
rejoicing in the inhabited world,
and delighting in the human race.

(Adapted from Proverbs 8:27–31)

Closing prayer: Give us wisdom to exult in your presence, to dance together in your joy, and to delight in all the pleasures of creation.

✧ **Meditation 6** ✧

God in Grief

Theme: Even a strong faith cannot protect us from the devastating grief of the loss of a loved one. At these times we are most aware of God in God's seeming absence.

Opening prayer: We bring our sorrow, our wounds, and our losses to you, God of eternal life.

About Lewis

In 1952, Lewis met Helen Joy Davidman, an American from New York City, a writer, a convert to Christianity from atheism, and a former active member of the Communist Party in the United States. They were married in a civil ceremony in 1956, and in a religious ceremony in 1957, a ceremony that had to take place in an Oxford hospital because Joy was being treated there for cancer.

It was feared that Joy would die that year, but she recovered briefly. She was well enough for the couple to make a trip to Ireland in 1958 and then to Greece in April 1960. She died in July that year.

Joy's death was a devastating blow that rocked Lewis to his very core. His belief in the loving will of God was put to an excruciating test. "You never know how much you really believe anything," wrote Lewis, "until its truth or falsehood becomes a matter of life and death to you" (*A Grief Observed*, p. 21).

Lewis did not find any comfort in the saying that his beloved would live on in his memory:

> What pitiable cant to say "She will live forever in my memory!" *Live?* That is exactly what she won't do. You might as well think like the old Egyptians that you can keep the dead by embalming them. (*A Grief Observed*, p. 19)

For Lewis, the grief over Joy's death was stark and without any obvious exit. In an effort to describe his anguish, Lewis wrote:

> You want her with all her resistances, all her faults, all her unexpectedness. That is, in her foursquare and independent reality. And this, not any image or memory, is what we are to love still, after she is dead. (*A Grief Observed*, p. 52)

Pause: Recall the hardest loss in your own life.

Lewis's Words

> Where is God? This is one of the most disquieting symptoms. When you are happy, so happy that you have no sense of needing Him, so happy that you are tempted to feel His claims upon you as an interruption, if you remember yourself and turn to Him with gratitude and praise, you will be—or so it feels—welcomed with open arms. But go to Him when your need is desperate, when all other help is vain, and what do you find? A door slammed in your face, and a sound of bolting and double bolting on the inside. After that, silence. You may as well turn away. The longer you wait, the more emphatic the silence will become. There are no lights in the windows. It might be an empty house. Was it ever inhabited? It seemed so once. And that seeming was as strong as this. What can this mean? Why is he so present a commander

in our time of prosperity and so very absent a help in time of trouble?

I tried to put some of these thoughts to C. this afternoon. He reminded me that the same thing seems to have happened to Christ: "Why hast thou forsaken me?" I know. Does that make it easier to understand? (C. S. Lewis, *A Grief Observed*, p. 9)

Reflection

Lewis held that grief, sadness, the loss of someone to death or betrayal or chance, and the apparent silence of God must be lived as authentically and spiritually as any moment of God-given pleasure. One must not avert one's gaze from the deepest losses each of us either has faced or will yet have to endure.

Lewis experienced the price for loving another person—a thoroughgoing vulnerability. This was the cost of the incarnation of God's love in Christ. And yet Christ's suffering does not eclipse or erase our own suffering. Indeed, the starkness of death may be something that we especially need to feel if we are to believe in more than death. The death of a person is the cutting short of something that cannot be exhausted. We might be able to speak of the exhausting of something physical or the completion of some activity, but there is something cruel and wrong about thinking that one can ever exhaust or be finished with a person.

Being severed from another person by their death leaves us feeling abandoned, hopeless, and without any reference point. Without a full sense of the horror of such loss, we cannot duly appreciate the hope that we have in a God who defeats death.

✧ If you are presently grieving, pray your sorrow with the following psalm:

Yahweh, hear my prayer;
let my cry for help come to you.

Since I am in trouble,
do not conceal your face from me.
Turn and listen to me.
When I call, respond to me quickly.
For my days are vanishing like smoke,
my bones burn like fire,
my heart withers like scorched grass;
even my appetite is gone.
And when I sigh,
my skin clings to my bones.
I am like a pelican living in the wilderness,
or a screech owl haunting the ruins.
I lie awake moaning
like some lonely bird on the rooftops.

. . . .

The bread I eat has become like ashes;
what I drink is mixed with my tears—

. . . .

My days pass away like shadows;
I wither away like grass.
But you, Yahweh, endure forever.

(Psalm 102:1–12)

✧ Make yourself present to someone who is suffering a loss from death.

✧ Create a package that symbolizes the greatest losses you have suffered or are suffering now. Tie this package up with a ribbon of your chosen color and set it in a visible place in your residence. When you notice it during the day, prayerfully invite God's presence into your memories, asking God to heal wounds, restore health, and be with the living and the dead.

✧ Meditating on the following "God's Word" section, enter into the bewilderment of the women who witnessed Christ's death and experienced the empty tomb.

God's Word

And very early on the first day of the week, when the sun had risen, [Mary Magdalene, Mary the mother of James, and Salome] went to the tomb [of Jesus]. They had been saying to one another, "Who will roll away the stone for us from the entrance to the tomb?" When they looked up, they saw that the stone, which was very large, had already been rolled back. As they entered the tomb, they saw a young man, dressed in a white robe, sitting on the right side; and they were alarmed. But he said to them, "Do not be alarmed; you are looking for Jesus of Nazareth, who was crucified. He has been raised; he is not here. Look, there is the place they laid him. But go, tell his disciples and Peter that he is going ahead of you to Galilee; there you will see him, just as he told you." So they went out and fled from the tomb, for terror and amazement had seized them; and they said nothing to anyone, for they were afraid. (Mark 16:2–8)

Closing prayer: By your cross and your Resurrection, you have set us free. You are the Savior of the world.

✧ Meditation 7 ✧

Friendships in God

Theme: Faithful friends are a gift of God that we should nourish and for which we should give thanks.

Opening prayer: Holy God, we thank you for the friendships of this life. Assist us in fidelity and hope in these bonds of love.

About Lewis

Lewis, with his keen intellect and lively feeling for human relationships, wrote a book entitled *The Four Loves,* which he defined as affection, friendship, eros, and agape. About friends, he said:

> Friends are not primarily absorbed in each other. It is when we are doing things together that friendship springs up—painting, sailing ships, praying, philosophizing, fighting shoulder to shoulder. Friends look in the same direction. Lovers look at each other: that is, in opposite directions. (C. S. Lewis, *Present Concerns,* p. 20)

Throughout his life Lewis enjoyed having good friends. From the late 1930s and through the 1950s, Lewis and a group of his friends met on Tuesday mornings and Thursday evenings to discuss literary works. The gaiety, humor, and festivity of such meetings defined much of what Lewis described as his happiest and most intellectually stimulating exchanges. They sometimes met in a pub in Oxford called The Eagle and the Child (nicknamed The Bird and the Baby), which today displays a sign to commemorate these gatherings. The group consisted of Christian artists and intellectuals, including J. R. R. Tolkien and Charles Williams.

Williams had a powerful effect on Lewis's life. Lewis found him to be a loving, gracious, and highly gifted companion. In an affectionate description of Williams, Lewis said of him:

> His face was thought ugly: I am not sure that the word "monkey" has not been murmured in this context. But the moment he spoke it became, as was also said, like the face of an angel . . . a spirit burning with intelligence and charity. (*Essays Presented to Charles Williams*, p. xiv)

In company with Williams, the poet W. H. Auden reported that he felt

> "for the first time in my life . . . in the presence of personal sanctity." . . .
> "I had met many good people before who made me feel ashamed of my own shortcomings, but in the presence of this man—we never discussed anything but literary business—I did not feel ashamed. I felt transformed into a person who was incapable of doing or thinking anything base or unloving." (Humphrey Carpenter, *W. H. Auden*, p. 224)

Lewis's experience was the very same. And so the sense of loss at Williams's death in 1945 was tremendous. In this Lewis came to sense the enduring nature of love on both sides of the grave:

> No event has so corroborated my faith in the next world as Williams did simply by dying. When the idea of death and the idea of Williams thus met in my mind, it was the idea of death that was changed. (*Essays Presented to Charles Williams*, p. xiv)

Pause: Bring to mind and heart your closest friend or friends and their gifts. What would be missed if they were not in your life?

Lewis's Words

Some of you may feel that this [transformational change] is very unlike your own experience. You may say "I've never had the sense of being helped by an invisible Christ, but I often have been helped by other human beings." That is rather like the woman in the first war who said that if there were a bread shortage it would not bother her house because they always ate toast. If there is no bread there will be no toast. If there were no help from Christ, there would be no help from other human beings. He works on us in all sorts of ways: not only through what we think our "religious life." He works through Nature, through our own bodies, through books, sometimes through experiences which seem (at the time) *anti*-Christian. . . . But above all, He works on us through each other. (C. S. Lewis, *Mere Christianity*, p. 148)

Reflection

It is a challenge to maintain a universal love and to "love your neighbor as yourself," and yet to allow the deep and enduring attraction of "this particular person" or "this particular group" to have its day. Yet, the Scriptures portray Christ himself as having a group of disciples, with some chosen for special roles. The fourth Gospel highlights the beloved disciple, Jesus' friends at Bethany, and the importance of Mary Magdalene after Jesus' death. The God of the Gospels is a God of all life that desires the cultivation of friendships among and for each child of God.

For Lewis, the pleasure in friendship is a mirror of the diversity and unity of life. He did not see his friend as an extension of himself but as someone different, and someone to be loved for that difference. The greatest enemy of friendship is self-absorbed pride:

Pride is the movement whereby a creature (that is, an essentially dependent being whose principle of existence lies not in itself but in another) tries to set up on its own, to exist for itself. (C. S. Lewis, *The Problem of Pain*, p. 75)

In Lewis's reciprocal relationship with Joy, he shared with one and the same person affection, eros, friendship, and agape. The most precious gift that friendship with Joy and their marriage gave to Lewis was the continual impact of something intimate and close, and yet at the same time unmistakably other, resistant, real.

✧ Do you have any group of friends that you should take the initiative to gather together regularly? Make your list, and get on the phone or e-mail today.

✧ Reflect on the "God's Word" section. Meditate in thanksgiving about the most significant persons in your life. Do something today to show your care and concern for them.

✧ Make a list of friends that you want to pray for. Create your own plan to use this list in prayer.

✧ When Lewis discovered that his own list of people to pray for was too long or outdated, he was reluctant to scratch their names off. He trusted the fact that if he fixed his mind on God, the right people would pop into his mind. Using this exercise, gently ponder and pray for those who appear during your prayer time.

✧ Write a letter to C. S. Lewis, expressing your thoughts and reactions to the following saying of his:

Where men are forbidden to honour a king they honour millionaires, athletes, or film-stars instead: even famous prostitutes or gangsters. For spiritual nature, like bodily nature, will be served; deny it food and it will gobble poison. (C. S. Lewis, *Present Concerns*, p. 20)

God's Word

Faithful friends are a sturdy shelter:
    whoever finds one has found a treasure.
Faithful friends are beyond price;
    no amount can balance their worth.
Faithful friends are life-saving medicine;
    and those who fear the Lord will find them.
Those who fear the Lord direct their friendship aright,
    for as they are, so are their neighbors also.

(Sirach 6:14–17)

Closing prayer: Be near at hand, O Holy God, and up-
hold us all in your loving embrace. Bring us and all those
whose lives are linked with ours ever more deeply into your
presence.

✧ Meditation 8 ✧

Families in God

Theme: Lewis believed in the importance of families. When he married Joy Davidman, he came to appreciate even more the love between husband and wife and family as divine gifts.

Opening prayer: Visit us, O Holy Spirit, with the gift of enduring, passionate love.

About Lewis

Lewis learned the fragile nature of family life early. His mother died when he was nine years old. This event recast the young boy's life: "All that was tranquil and reliable disappeared from my life. . . . It was sea and islands now" (C. S. Lewis, *Surprised by Joy*, p. 21).

Lewis was alienated for a time from his father because he could not endure the style of his father's communication, his inability to listen, and his ponderous approach to the affairs of the day. But as a more matured son, Jack seemed to be reconciled to his father during his father's last years. In fact, because of Warren's absence in the military, it was Jack who took care of their father's affairs during his final illness and upon his death.

Jack Lewis and his brother, Warren, bonded during their boyhood, enjoying days in the attic with their pencils, paper, and paints, writing and illustrating stories woven from their imaginations. Their relationship endured as a true brother-hood all through their adult lives. For most of his adult life, Lewis lived singly, sharing his house, the Kilns, with Warren.

His love for and marriage to Joy Davidman brought Lewis a new understanding of the goodness and sadness of love and family. When Joy died Lewis wrote:

> Her absence is like the sky, spread over everything.
> But no, that is not quite accurate. There is one place where her absence comes locally home to me, and it is a place I can't avoid. I mean my own body. It had such a different importance while it was the body of H's lover. Now it's like an empty house. (*A Grief Observed*, p. 13)

Family was a wonderful gift, of course, but it was also the source of his great suffering. Lewis bewailed: "Cancer, and cancer, and cancer. My mother, my father, my wife. I wonder who is next in the queue" (*A Grief Observed*, p. 14).

While Lewis treasured his loves, he also keenly realized the peril of elevating a family or family life into an idol or a false god. "Love, having become a god, becomes a demon" (C. S. Lewis, *The Four Loves*, p. 83). He recognized the tyranny that can be operative in domestic life, and he recounted one of its forms in a humorous way:

> Erected by her sorrowing brothers
> In memory of Martha Clay.
> Here lies one who lived for others;
> Now she has peace. And so have they.
> (C. S. Lewis, *Poems*, p. 134)

Lewis often linked his treatment of family and of eros. His measurement of both is similar. Family and eros are to be valued and weighed in the great context of a God-filled life, and not seen as supremely private matters in which anything goes. The loss of a greater framework can turn the gifts of family and eros into a profoundly dark, lethal trap.

Pause: Ask yourself: What part has eros played in my life of love? In my relationship with God? In the life of my present family?

Lewis's Words

It is in the grandeur of Eros that the seeds of danger are concealed. He has spoken like a god. His total commitment, his reckless disregard of happiness, his transcendence of self-regard, sound like a message from the eternal world.

And yet it cannot, just as it stands, be the voice of God Himself. For Eros, speaking with that very grandeur and displaying that very transcendence of self, may urge to evil as well as to good. Nothing is shallower than the belief that a love which leads to sin is always qualitatively lower—more animal or more trivial—than one which leads to faithful, fruitful and Christian marriage. The love which leads to cruel and perjured unions, even to suicide-pacts and murder, is not likely to be wandering lust or idle sentiment. It may well be Eros in all his splendour; heartbreakingly sincere; ready for every sacrifice except renunciation. (C. S. Lewis, *The Four Loves*, p. 151)

Reflection

If everything is open to God's gaze—and more important, to God's love—then one cannot seal off sections of life as absolutely private and isolated from God. This means that the personal relations of family and romance cannot be taken as constituting a space entirely free of virtue and divine counsel. In the most intimate family and romantic relations, Lewis believes that we have the opportunity to magnify God, to reverence the shared relationship in God, or to harm one another. By inviting God into these relations, we do not open ourselves up to some alien force, a foreign power. Rather, we are to welcome the Creator, who fashioned us as persons capable of profound intimacy.

Lewis's caution about eros is, in a sense, a high compliment to its power and its fitting, wonderful place in a God-centered life. In a sense he had a higher view of eros than those who shun discussion of it and leave it all to private, individual deliberation. While Lewis was wary of eros that could not endure renunciation, and family relations that were severed from responsibility, he had no patience with a Christianity that treated eros as shameful or family life as inferior to a life of solitude. In his view, a mature and authentic Christian spirituality dispels the hatred of one's own body, family, and community. In fact, the Christian life enhances and stabilizes the sensitivity to our body, family, and community.

✧ Where in my family life do I confront
+ my temper?
+ my moodiness?
+ my reluctance to share with others?
+ my self-centered ambitions?

Examine your conscience in regard to these. Reflect on the situations in which they are most manifest. Pray for the grace of forgiveness and healing. Choose one area that is the most troublesome and imagine the attitude and action that would serve as its antidote. Invite the Holy Spirit to help you in this examination.

✧ Identify in writing some public events in which eros was manifested as tyrannical and fanatical (suicides, murders, and so on). Write down your own thoughts about these events and what you think might have prevented these eruptions or might have better channeled this energy.

✧ What advice would you give to a young person who is caught in the throes of erotic love? After meditating and praying over this question, write down in a letter everything that you think needs to be said. Review the letter after a week. Ask yourself, Would anyone I know profit from this letter?

✧ Read the "God's Word" section and reflect on the following comment by Lewis, "When I have learnt to love God better than my earthly dearest, I shall love my earthly dearest better than I do now" (W. H. Lewis, ed., *Letters*, p. 248). Make up your own prayer for an increase of love.

God's Word

[Jesus said:] Whoever loves father or mother more than me is not worthy of me; and whoever loves son or daughter more than me is not worthy of me; and whoever does not take up the cross and follow me is not worthy of me. Those who find their life will lose it, and those who lose their life for my sake will find it. (Matthew 10:37–39)

Closing prayer: O God, we thank you for the gift of our family and the gift of love. Bless, hallow, and magnify our earthly loves in your great goodness.

Work in God's World

Theme: Our work is called forth by God for the building up of the people of God and all creation.

Opening prayer: Gracious God, thank you for the talents you have given us and the command to use them. Enable us to create environments and lives that allow these talents to flourish for the good of all your people.

About Lewis

Lewis was steadily employed throughout his adult life. However, despite the prestige of his Oxford position and his immense popularity among students and the general public, Lewis had some difficulties holding the professional respect of his colleagues. In the late 1940s and early 1950s, he was repeatedly passed over for various positions in the Oxford community. One widely circulated reason for this was Lewis's public identity as a Christian writer.

Lewis's popular religious writing was deemed unfitting for a scholar by some of his secular colleagues. One of his contemporaries comments on Lewis's predicament:

> The academic mind is a master of the politely barbed shaft. The college (that Lewis belonged to) was pervaded

by an abrasive anti-Christian humanism at that time, which gave Lewis a good deal of painful opposition. (Como, ed., *C. S. Lewis at the Breakfast Table,* p. 226)

Eventually a chair of medieval and Renaissance English at Cambridge University was offered to him, which he accepted in 1954.

Lewis's novels, such as *That Hideous Strength,* contain trenchant criticism of inhuman institutions. In this novel Lewis depicts a macabre corporation (the National Institute of Co-ordinated Experiments, or N.I.C.E.) wedded to an impersonal view of nature and humanity. To N.I.C.E, "nature is something dead—a machine to be worked, and taken to bits if it won't work the way he pleases" (*That Hideous Strength,* p. 336).

It is possible that much of Lewis's experience of academic competition, infighting, and the common desperate effort to be in the inner circle contributed to the message in this book. It also may have influenced his fantasized portrait of hell in his book *The Screwtape Letters,* in which hell is a massive bureaucracy turned in upon itself. In this mock institution, Lewis humorously and incisively displays the awful consequence of unfettered self-interest. Lewis thought it was important for respect and dignity to pervade the workplace, so that the persons working might exercise their talents and the fruits of their labor might be in harmony with the greater workings of God.

Pause: Ask yourself, What is my main work and what are its fruits?

Lewis's Words

It is no disparagement to a garden to say that it will not fence and weed itself, nor prune its own fruit trees, nor roll and cut its own lawns. A garden is a good thing but that is not the sort of goodness it has. It will remain a garden, as distinct from a wilderness, only if someone does all these things to it. Its real glory is of quite a different kind. The very fact that it needs constant weeding and pruning bears witness to that glory. It teems with life. It glows with colour and smells like heaven and puts forward at every hour of a summer day beauties which man could never have created and could not even, on his own resources, have imagined. If you want to see the difference between its contribution and the gardener's, put the commonest weed it grows side by side with his hoes, rakes, shears, and packet of weed killer; you have put beauty, energy and fecundity beside dead, sterile things. Just so, our "decency and common sense" show grey and deathlike beside the geniality of love. And when the garden is in its full glory the gardener's contributions to that glory will still have been in a sense paltry compared with those of nature. Without life springing from the earth, without rain, light and heat descending from the sky, he could do nothing. When he has done all, he has merely encouraged here and discouraged there, powers and beauties that have a different source. But his share, though small, is indispensable and laborious. When God planted a garden He set a man over it and set the man under Himself. When He planted the garden of our nature and caused the flowering, fruiting loves to grow there, He set our will to "dress" them. Compared with them it is dry and cold. And unless His grace comes down, like the rain and the sunshine, we shall use this tool to little purpose. But its laborious—and largely negative—services are indispensable. (C. S. Lewis, *The Four Loves*, pp. 163–164)

Reflection

A principle that runs through almost all of C. S. Lewis's spirituality is that all our fundamental abilities come from God and their flourishing and fruitfulness are to be found principally in relation to God. It is from the standpoint of being blessed as God's creatures that we are to understand our whole life, including our work. Also, when we try to bury these talents and squelch their use in ourselves or in others, we court profound dangers. Self-centered individualism in relation to God-given talents can undo our work and undermine the workplace.

By insisting on the good of shared labor and the foolishness of selfish preoccupation, Lewis insisted on the responsibility to work for equitable, dignified employment and to challenge unjust institutions. Those of us who are employed need to pray and work so that those who are unemployed may have new and fruitful opportunities to work. Those of us who are unemployed must seek out opportunities for a work life or a life of activity in whatever way God ordains and pray that God will keep us confident and trusting in this search.

✦ Lewis lived through a difficult transition in the move from Oxford to Cambridge. Reflect on your own security or precarity in your work situation. Should you be doing something for yourself or others? Do you know a person who needs your support in a time of transition? Plan to contribute to your local food bank or clothing center, goods—fruits of your labor—that will help others in a time of need.

✦ If the season allows, go out and work in a garden. Take a few minutes to regard the fecund earth before you and the lifeless tools you are going to use. While gardening, just enjoy it. When you are finished, take care of your aching body and your dirty hands and offer a prayer of gratitude for this kind of work.

✦ "Our 'decency and common sense' show grey and deathlike beside the geniality of love." Use this reflection to think about your daily work:
+ What dimensions of your work seem boring, grey, and deathlike?
+ Are these dimensions truly deadening to yourself or to others?
+ Are these boring dimensions just a facet of common sense and decency, that is, are they factors of truly humane work that are beneficial to a larger community?

✦ Are you able to consider yourself a person of common sense and decency in your work and work environment?

✦ Does your work allow you to experience at times "the geniality of love"?

Renew your commitment to your work, or plan to make changes that will renew your integrity.

✧ Consider someone at your workplace who seems to be disheartened or isolated. Plan to do some act that will make their time at work more pleasant, such as bringing flowers or snacks or sharing a coffee break with them. Lift up these acts to God in silence, praying that God will bless this person and the colleagues around them.

✧ Open the Scriptures to Matthew 25:14–30 and read the parable of the talents. Consider the gifts and talents that you have been given and your response to them. Pray for the grace of increased initiative and for confidence in your work.

God's Word

"O God of my ancestors and Lord of mercy,
With you is wisdom, she who knows your works
and was present when you made the world;
. . . .
Send her forth from the holy heavens,
and from the throne of your glory send her,
that she may labor at my side,
and that I may learn what is pleasing to you.
For she knows and understands all things,
and she will guide me wisely in my actions
and guard me with her glory.
Then my works will be acceptable,
and I shall judge your people justly,
and shall be worthy of the throne of my father."
(Wisdom of Solomon 9:1,9–12)

Closing prayer: Bless, O God, the work of our hands, and help us to place that work, and our very selves, in your care.

✧ **Meditation 10** ✧

The Great Miracle

Theme: Our redemption lies in Christ.

Opening prayer: Save us, O God, so that we might be made whole.

About Lewis

Lewis held that in Christ we see the central liberating action of God, an action with cosmic and daily reverberations. In the 1930s he came to believe in the historical reality of the Divine Incarnation of God in the life of Jesus Christ. From then on Lewis's speeches and writings show a new awareness that the event of Christ's God-human embodiment has a saving force with profound existential meaning.

Central to Lewis's later writing is the thesis that humans cannot save themselves. Evil threatens to entangle us like a snare or an addiction. Bad habits, small sins—the odd malicious comment, the snubbing of a friend, the neglect of those in need—conspire to encase humanity in a joyless grip. Human efforts to break free are too often fruitless, either because of a lack of power or because the very effort to free ourselves reinforces a deadening self-preoccupation.

In Lewis's children's story *The Lion, the Witch and the Wardrobe*, he charmingly and very simply represents what it is like to fall captive to an overwhelming force. One of the lads, Edmund, becomes ridiculously fixated on Turkish Delight candy, and for the sake of this absurd addiction, lies to and betrays his brother and sisters. In the same book, with the figure of the lion Aslan, Lewis offers an imaginative picture of the essential Christian teaching: that God in Christ took on the forces of darkness by bearing the brunt of suffering and hate and then breaking free of death through the absolute power of divine love.

Humanity is liberated by Christ's action. Participating in this saving action requires a deliberate passivity on our part, a genuine openness to a life-offering movement on God's part. Our healing and deliverance from evil is to be marked by our uniting ourselves to Christ. Christ's life and teaching are to shape our character, while faith in Christ's Resurrection is to define our faith in God's transforming power. The Resurrection is not about the resuscitation of a corpse or the recuperation of someone who has been ill; it is about a radical, life-centered transfiguration or translation. "'What are we to make of Christ?' There is no question of what we can make of Him, it is entirely a question of what He intends to make of us" (C. S. Lewis, *God in the Dock*, p. 160).

Pause: What is Christ making of you?

Lewis's Words

The perfect surrender and humiliation were undergone by Christ: perfect because He was God, surrender and humiliation because He was man. Now the Christian belief is that if we somehow share the humility and suffering of Christ we shall also share in His conquest of death and find a new life after we have died and in it become perfect, and perfectly happy, creatures. This means something much more than our trying to follow His teaching. People often ask when the next step in evolution—the step to something beyond man—will happen. But on the

Christian view, it has happened already. In Christ a new kind of man appeared: and the new kind of life which began in Him is to be put into us. (C. S. Lewis, *Mere Christianity*, p. 52)

Most certainly, beyond all worlds, unconditioned and unimaginable, transcending discursive thought, there yawns forever the ultimate Fact, the fountain of all other facthood, the burning and undiminished depth of the Divine Life. Most certainly also, to be united with that Life in the eternal Sonship of Christ is, strictly speaking, the only thing worth a moment's consideration. And in so far as *that* is what you mean by *Heaven*, Christ's divine Nature never left it, and therefore never returned to it: and His human nature ascended thither not at the moment of the Ascension but at every moment. . . . I allow and insist that the Eternal Word, the Second Person of the Trinity, can never be, nor have been, confined to any place at all: it is rather in Him that all places exist. (C. S. Lewis, *Miracles*, p. 161)

Reflection

The Incarnation is paradoxical: in finite life one can discover infinite life; in calmly resting in Christ, one can be radically transformed and caught up in a greater divine movement. Christ is wholly God, not the whole of God; Christ is not the eternal Father and not the Holy Spirit.

The key to sharing in the saving work of the Incarnation involves letting go, releasing the self-involved emotions of fear and timidity, and detaching from the works they bring forth. It involves the cultivation of a life-giving reliance on Christ amid the paradoxes. In particular, Lewis's devotion to the Incarnation meant a devotion to be wholly given over to God, and to do so not in a piecemeal, naive fashion but in concrete ways—intellectually, emotionally, and in action. The action may be costly, and yet as Lewis learned in various struggles, God's love leaves no alternative:

To love at all is to be vulnerable. . . . The alternative to tragedy, or at least to the risk of tragedy, is damnation. The only place outside Heaven where you can be perfectly safe from all the dangers and perturbations of love is Hell. (C. S. Lewis, *The Four Loves*, p. 169)

✧ Without the goodwill and cooperation of others, our life would be threadbare. All these goods, passively received, may provide a picture of the greater good offered to us continually in a growing relation to Christ. Ponder many of the ways in which our life is good because of our trust and passive reliance on others.

✧ Offer a prayer of thanksgiving for the significant persons whom you trust, on whose goodness you rely, and who provide for you in ways you cannot provide for yourself.

✧ Seated before a crucifix, ponder the body that is on it. It is Christ's suffering that convicts us of our own ills and exhibits the consequences of wrongdoing. Reflect on your own suffering from sin, either sins you have committed or sins you have endured. Allow the feelings of sorrow and repentance to surface. Unite your feelings to the Christ figure before you.

✧ Are there works of repentance and reparation that you need to perform today?

✧ God can bring good out of evil. Reflect on times and events in which you have encountered a true good that has come out of a truly grievous evil.

✧ Awaken yourself before sunrise, and sit quietly awaiting the dawning of a new day. When the light has come, say a prayer of praise as you move into the day.

God's Word

In the beginning was the Word, and the Word was with God, and the Word was God. He was in the beginning with God. All things came into being through him, and without him not one thing came into being. What has come into being in him was life, and the life was the light of all people. The light shines in the darkness and the darkness did not overcome it. . . .

He was in the world, and the world came into being through him; yet the world did not know him. . . . But to all who received him, who believed in his name, he gave power to become children of God. . . .

And the Word became flesh and lived among us, and we have seen his glory, the glory as of a father's only son, full of grace and truth. (John 1:1–14)

Closing prayer: Into your hands, O God, I commend my spirit.

✧ Meditation 11 ✧

Descent and Re-ascent

Theme: Life in Christ involves a sacred and life-affirming rhythm of descending and re-ascending.

Opening prayer: We thank you, O God, for the rhythms of life that manifest your great power and goodness.

About Lewis

At the bottom of the hill near the Kilns, where Lewis lived, was a pond that formed when the clay had been taken for brickmaking. Lewis often went swimming there. He rowed a small boat out to the middle, tied it to a protruding stump, and plunged in. Later, when speaking of the Incarnation, Lewis wrote:

> In the Christian story God descends to re-ascend. He comes down; down from the heights of absolute being into time and space, down into humanity; down further still, if embryologists are right, to recapitulate in the womb ancient and pre-human phases of life: down to the very roots and sea-bed of the Nature He has created. But He goes down to come up again and bring the whole ruined world up with Him. One has the picture of a strong

man stooping lower and lower to get himself underneath some great complicated burden. . . . Or one may think of a diver, first reducing himself to nakedness, then glancing in mid-air, then gone with a splash, vanished, rushing down through green and warm water into black and cold water, down through increasing pressure into the death-like region of ooze and slime and old decay; then up again, back to colour and light, his lungs almost bursting, till suddenly he breaks surface again, holding in his hand the dripping, precious thing that he went down to recover. He and it are both coloured now that they have come up into the light: down below, where it lay colourless in the dark, he lost his colour too. (*Miracles*, pp. 111–112)

Pause: Ask yourself, When have I had the experience of diving deep and re-ascending to the light?

Lewis's Words

In this descent and re-ascent everyone will recognise a familiar pattern: a thing written all over the world. It is the pattern of all vegetable life. It must belittle itself into something hard, small and deathlike, it must fall into the ground: thence a new life re-ascends. It is the pattern of all animal generation too. There is the descent from the full and perfect organisms into the spermatozoon and ovum, and in the dark womb a life at first inferior in kind to that of the species which is being reproduced: then the slow ascent to the perfect embryo, to the living, conscious baby, and finally to the adult. So it is also in our moral and emotional life. The first innocent and spontaneous desires have to submit to the deathlike process of control or total denial: but from that there is a re-ascent to fully formed character in which the strength of the original material all operates but in a new way. Death and Re-birth— go down to go up—it is a key principle. Through this bottleneck, this belittlement, the highroad nearly always lies.

The doctrine of the Incarnation, if accepted, puts this principle even more emphatically at the centre. The pattern is there in Nature because it was first there in God. All the instances of it which I have mentioned turn out to be but transpositions of the Divine theme into a minor key. (C. S. Lewis, *Miracles*, pp. 116–117)

Reflection

Lewis was keenly aware of the cost of God's meeting us in the Incarnation and of us meeting one another in Christ. This undergirded his affirmation of the joy of Christianity in its depth and complexity. Christianity holds out for a high, merry conclusion of life in a joyful reconciliation, or meeting, with God, but it is one that is achieved through continual rhythms of death and rebirth.

In his children's stories, Lewis often used play as a central image of reconciliation and fulfillment. Consider two insights about games and how these may signal something about the play and joy in meeting one another in the life God has given us. A game, of any sort, is a manifestation of the simple, ordinary rhythms of life; yet, when well-played with strength and spontaneity, it brings a satisfaction to oneself, a communion with others, and a further openness to life. The second insight is the recognition that each game demands something of us: preparation, discipline of body and mind, willingness to function as a team, the ability to lose, the possibility of playing badly. And no game is final.

✧ Spend some time today at play: engage in your favorite sport, play a game with children. Enjoy the discipline and the spontaneity.

✧ Find an icon or a holy image and spend time before it contemplating the unity of the divine and human natures in Christ.

✧ Reread the "Lewis's Words" section. Write about the movements of your life (physical, emotional, intellectual, or moral) that have called for a deathlike descent and then a re-ascent.

✧ Identify one "precious thing" you have brought up out of the muck of life. Use some modeling clay to represent this precious thing in a new form. Keep it in a spot where it will recall its meaning for you, or pass it on to someone who would appreciate it.

God's Word

But each of us was given grace according to the measure of Christ's gift. Therefore it is said, "When he ascended on high he made captivity itself a captive; / he gave gifts to his people." (When it says, "He ascended," what does it mean but that he had also descended into the lower parts of the earth. He who descended is the same one who ascended far above all the heavens, so that he might fill all things.) (Ephesians 4:7–10)

Closing prayer: O God, we thank you for entering into our life and taking it to yourself. We praise you for the rhythms that you have placed in all creation. May we continue to ascend, until we see you face-to-face.

The God Behind Our Idea of God

Theme: Let God be God.

Opening prayer: O God, breaker of idols, descend into our heart and mind so that we may know you and love you ever more and more.

About Lewis

Lewis fostered a lively intellectual community in Oxford, the Socratic Club, in which Christian and non-Christian intellectuals met to debate the significance and truth of religious beliefs. Some of the atheist and agnostic philosophers who came to these meetings were among the most prestigious philosophers in the English-speaking world. These meetings were lively and often involved the sharp exchanges that mark fierce intellectual debate.

If it were a matter of winning and losing, then it appears the Christians did not always win. At one point Lewis observed: "'At the Socratic the enemy often wipe the floor with us'" (Como, ed., *C. S. Lewis at the Breakfast Table*, p. 21). Even so, Lewis relished the opportunity to articulate and defend Christian belief and to do so with intelligence and humor.

His resilience appears to have come from his belief that, in the end, God, not philosophy or intellectual sport, is the enduring object of hope. "'We have no abiding city even in philosophy: all passes except the Word'" (Como, ed., *C. S. Lewis at the Breakfast Table*, p. 22).

Trust in God and a wry hesitation to fully trust himself gave Lewis intellectual humility and courage: "My idea of God is not a divine idea. It has to be shattered time after time." Lewis thought this breaking up and reshaping of his view of God was just what he should expect. He believed that his ideas of God were sometimes broken by God: "[God] is the great iconoclast. Could we not say that this shattering is one of the marks of His presence?" (C. S. Lewis, *A Grief Observed*, p. 52).

Pause: When has God shattered your idea and image of God?

Lewis's Words

All reality is iconoclastic. The earthly beloved, even in this life, incessantly triumphs over your mere idea of her. And you want her to; you want her with all her resistances, all her faults, all her unexpectedness. That is, in her foursquare and independent reality. (C. S. Lewis, *A Grief Observed*, p. 52)

We must beware of the Past, mustn't we? I mean that any fixing of the mind on old evils beyond what is absolutely necessary for repenting our own sins and forgiving those of others is certainly useless and usually bad for us. Notice in Dante that the lost souls are entirely concerned with their past! Not so the saved. This is one of the dangers of being, like you and me, old. There's so much past, now, isn't there? And so little else. But we must try very hard not to keep on endlessly chewing the cud. We must look forward more eagerly to sloughing that old skin off forever. (C. S. Lewis, *Letters to an American Lady*, pp. 98–99)

Reflection

For Christian intellectuals and scholars, there can be a particularly alluring danger in trusting too much in one's own ideas of God and not enough in the reality behind the ideas, that reality to which one owes not just honor, allegiance, and devotion but one's very life. The teaching that the Incarnate Word is the mediator between God and creation may have to be realized even within our own consciousness, in which the Word must shatter, redeem, and refine the relation between us and our ideas about God.

Lewis opposed not just worldly vanity but intellectual vanity as well. For him, it is a good thing when ideas of God are roughed up in debate, lest we mistake our ideas of God for the reality of the God we worship. Intellectual debate, entered into humbly and openly, can enable us to appreciate that the greatness of God far outstrips our highest thoughts of God.

✧ Reread the second excerpt in the "Lewis's Words" section. A fixation on a past accomplishment or a "golden" period of one's early life can lead to spiritual sentimentality and atrophy. God is a living God who invites us to exercise stewardship over our memories. Respond to Lewis's letter with one of your own. Feel free to argue or disagree with him!

✧ Lewis was aware that in his relationship with Joy he had images of her, constructs about her in his mind, living memories that his own consciousness had formed. Yet her living "otherness" always shattered his ideas of her, much to his delight (or so he said!).

✧ Who is the person in your life who is most "iconoclastic"? What is your normal response to this? What can you do to more fully enjoy and appreciate the "otherness" of this person?

✧ G. K. Chesterton once advised that we not try to get heaven in our mind but that we strive instead to get our mind in heaven. What difference would it make in your thinking and imaging if you took this advice?

✧ Recite aloud several times the following poem by Lewis:

> All this is flashy rhetoric about loving you.
> I never had a selfless thought since I was born.
> I am mercenary and self-seeking through and through:
> I want God, you, all friends, merely to serve my turn.
>
> Peace, re-assurance, pleasure, are the goals I seek,
> I cannot crawl one inch outside my proper skin:
> I talk of Love—a scholar's parrot may talk Greek—
> But, self-imprisoned, always end where I begin.
>
> Only that now you have taught me (but how late) my
>   lack.
> I see the chasm. And everything you are was making
> My heart into a bridge by which I might get back
> From exile, and grow man. And now the bridge is
>   breaking.
>
> For this I bless you as the ruin falls. The pains
> You give me are more precious than all other gains.
>
> (C. S. Lewis, *Poems*, pp. 109–110)

God's Word

The days are surely coming
when I will make a new covenant
with the house of Israel and the house of Judah.
It will not be like the covenant I made with their ancestors.
This is the covenant that I will make in those days:
I will put my law within them,
and I will write it on their hearts;

and I will be their God,
and they shall be my people.

(Adapted from Jeremiah 31:31–33)

Jesus [is] the mediator of a new covenant. (Hebrews 12:24)

Closing prayer: Holy God, purify our heart and mind that we may approach you in truth.

✧　**Meditation 13**　✧

An Embodied Spirituality

Theme: The Incarnation requires an embodied, integrated spirituality of personal thought and action.

Opening prayer: Pour your grace into us, O life-giving God, that we may truly be the body of Christ.

About Lewis

Lewis was a man of enormous graciousness and charity. Such charity was financial when he began to have an income from his books. Lewis was wise enough about his own talents and temperament to establish a foundation to distribute charitable funds.

Lewis's own acts of charity were more personal. He gave of his time, intelligence, and friendly concern to countless people through correspondence. People wrote to him often for advice, and they received his written reply, as well as friendship, in response. One of his enduring gifts to later generations is his letters, many of which were collected by faithful friends and are now widely published.

Lewis embodied his Christian spirituality, not only by his hard work as a professor, author, and speaker but also by fostering personal interaction as opposed to institutional or impersonal benevolence. And it was through his personal charity and gracious style of interaction that he was able to be such a convincing witness of the open-ended communion between God and the world, a communion established in Jesus Christ.

The exquisite integration that Lewis achieved in his active life was due in part to the fact that he took the reality of the body, soul, and spirit; the visible and the invisible; the human and the divine; the natural and the supernatural with great seriousness. The wisdom lay in Lewis's seeing visible life as sanctified and upheld by a wider, deeper communion with Christ. Without God's continuing creative and generative activity, the visible world would cease to be. Without access to God through this world in religious experience, humans would be without spiritual moorings. The dual relation, or traffic, between these realities was the key to Lewis's spirituality of embodiment. It did not involve the mechanical application of a rule or the performance of an isolated feat. A friend comments on the wisdom found in Lewis's work, "Wisdom has to be read off the whole shape of his thought and is not one trick within it" (Como, ed., *C. S. Lewis at the Breakfast Table*, p. xxx).

Pause: How do you embody your spirituality?

Lewis's Words

Nature does not, in the long run, favour life. If Nature is all that exists—in other words, if there is no God and no life of some quite different sort somewhere outside Nature—then all stories will end in the same way: in a universe from which all life is banished without possibility of return. It will have been an accidental flicker, and there will be no one even to remember it. (C. S. Lewis, *Present Concerns*, p. 74)

You must have tasted, however briefly, the pure water from beyond the world before you can be distinctly conscious of the hot, salty tang of Nature's current. To treat her as God, or as Everything, is to lose the whole pith and pleasure of her. Come out, look back, and then you will see . . . this astonishing cataract of bears, babies, and bananas: this immoderate deluge of atoms, orchids, oranges, cancers, canaries, fleas, gases, tornadoes and toads. How could you ever have thought this was the ultimate reality? How could you ever have thought that it was merely a stage-set for the moral drama of men and women? She is herself. Offer her neither worship nor contempt. Meet her and know her. (C. S. Lewis, *Miracles*, p. 67)

Reflection

Lewis was firmly convinced that a sustained awareness of the greater scope of God's reality fosters and refines an energized, animated love of this world. This awareness is not a once-and-for-all, singular event requiring disembodied awe but a settled state of our souls, an awareness that marks our life as a whole. Consider an analogy with painting. Some painters will lay down a uniform color on their canvas, burnt umber for example, and then paint over it. Even when not apparent explicitly, the burnt umber will still affect and shift the colors layered on it. The sustained awareness of God similarly can affect and shift our thoughts and actions, even when it is not directly apparent. Lewis's counsel on securing this awareness of God is, in a sense, realizing that we cannot secure it on our own. The important factor is to remain open to God's movement, to use our God-given imagination to challenge our sometimes sedentary moods, and to act in the world in light of God's charity. Being in a living, mutual relationship requires appreciating and growing with change.

Action is pivotal in a life of visible and invisible communion. God's love for us requires a tangible response on our part—reaching out to our neighbor, sometimes simply making ourselves available to a person in need.

✧ Ponder some of the seed images that Christ uses in the parables.

✦ Mark 4:1–9, the parable of the sower
✦ Mark 4:26–29, the parable of the growing seed
✦ Mark 4:30–32, the parable of the mustard seed

Take time to illustrate the images that come to you, or write a short story as if you were the developing seed.

✧ Reread in the "Lewis's Words" section about the "astonishing cataract" and "immoderate deluge" of nature's goods. Sing a song celebrating nature's goods.

✧ Review your financial donations to churches, charities, or nonprofit organizations. Are they extensive enough? Are they given to effective projects or institutions? What is your current annual plan?

✧ Review your investment of personal energy: time, intelligence, concern, service activities. Who most needs them at this time of your life? Are any changes called for?

✧ What gifts do you have as a member of the body of Christ?

God's Word

Now you are the body of Christ and individually members of it. (1 Corinthians 12:27)

Closing prayer: Holy Christ, Incarnate Word, bless the works you have given us to do.

A Trinitarian Life

Theme: Our life, by the mystery of the Incarnation, has been assumed into the life of the Trinity.

Opening prayer: Lift us, O Holy God, into your presence.

About Lewis

Critics have noted that one of the extraordinary charms of Lewis's language is that he addresses abstract theological topics in concrete and sometimes quite ordinary terms. This is a feature, as well, of Chaucer and Spenser, authors that Lewis studied and taught. Indeed, Lewis's description of Spenser's prose has been used to describe his own:

> "His work is one, like a growing thing, a tree . . . with branches reaching to heaven and roots to hell. . . . And between these two extremes comes all the multiplicity of human life. . . . To read him is to grow in mental health." (Como, ed., *C. S. Lewis at the Breakfast Table*, p. xxxiv)

For Lewis, this joining together of the abstract and the concrete is no mere stylistic device. It reflects a theological conviction. His highest insight is that the fulfillment of our life involves an integration or a growing into the life of God. This belief permeated his actions, emotions, imagination, and thoughts, and thus it carried over into his writing.

In his final novel, *Till We Have Faces*, Lewis powerfully presents the following proposition: in order to see the face of the Divine, we ourselves must have a face. The search for God and for our own identity is, in the end, intimately interwoven.

Pause: God is our Creator, Redeemer, and Sanctifier. Ask yourself, How do I grasp the trinitarian life in my own?

Lewis's Words

The whole dance, or drama, or pattern of this three-Personal life is to be played out in each one of us: or (putting it the other way round) each one of us has got to enter that pattern, take his place in that dance. There is no other way to the happiness for which we were made. Good things as well as bad, you know, are caught by a kind of infection. If you want to get warm, you must stand near the fire: if you want to be wet you must get into the water. If you want joy, power, peace, eternal life, you must get close to, or even into, the thing that has them. They are not a sort of prizes which God could, if He chose, just hand out to anyone. They are a great fountain of energy and beauty spurting up at the very centre of reality. If you are close to it, the spray will wet you: if you are not, you will remain dry. Once a man is united to God, how could he not live forever? Once a man is separated from God, what can he do but wither and die? (C. S. Lewis, *Mere Christianity*, p. 137)

Reflection

The life and work of C. S. Lewis challenge our private self-image—the clinging to self-willed projects and the control we attempt to exercise in relationships. In all such affairs, Lewis desires our escape from egocentric acts and attitudes and, by the style, variety, and vivacity of his written work, invites us to engage in a spiritual journey even to a participation in the life of God.

The threefold life of God was vital to Lewis. This life was an eternal mystery of generation and inspiration, a super-abundance internal to the life of God. God's outward, external love manifest in creation and redemption is a sign of this abundant life and love. The Trinitarian God that Christianity proclaims is the source of all life that we know.

✧ Reread the "Lewis's Words" section. Plan to go dancing, swimming, or picnicking by a fountain if possible.

✧ "If you want joy, power, peace, eternal life, you must get close to, or even into, the thing that has them." Reflect on what or whom you need to get close to, in order to experience this life from God.

✧ Take time to read one of Lewis's imaginative stories. (See the "For Further Reading" section at the end of the book.) Enter into it with attention and feeling, letting it resonate with your own imagination. At the completion of the story, thank the Author of authors for this book.

✧ Approach the frontiers of your selfishness concerning your self-image, your private projects, or your human relationships. Enter into the fears that are present with you there. Talk with the Creator about where these fears come from, the Redeemer about how the Good News can save you from them, and the Sanctifier about the graces you need to be free from them.

God's Word

I am the vine, you are the branches. Those who abide in me and I in them bear much fruit, because apart from me you can do nothing. Whoever does not abide in me is thrown away like a branch and withers. . . . If you abide in me and my words abide in you, ask for whatever you wish, and it will be done for you. My Father is glorified

by this, that you bear much fruit and become my disciples. As the Father has loved me, so I have loved you;
abide in my love. . . . I have said these things to you so
that my joy may be in you, and that your joy may be complete. (John 15:5–11)

Closing prayer: O living God, draw us near to all things
that bear your energy and beauty. Unite us ever more closely
to you.

✧ Meditation 15 ✧

Awaiting the Resurrection

Theme: If we have died with Christ, we believe that we shall also rise with Christ.

Opening prayer: Be with us, Saving God, now and at the hour of our death.

About Lewis

Warren Lewis recounted the events of his mother's death, when both he and Jack were small boys:

> [My mother] died on my father's birthday. . . . There was a Shakespearean calendar hanging on the wall of the room where she died, and my father preserved for the rest of his life the leaf for that day, with its quotation: "Men must endure their going hence." (W. H. Lewis, ed., *Letters*, p. 3)

This Shakespearean theme hung over the lives of the Lewis family for many years.

When C. S. Lewis later commented on his World War I experience, he suggested that one of the grim truths that came from it was the vivid reminder that all humans are mortal, a fact often far removed from consciousness during nonwar times.

As Lewis accepted Christianity for this life, he also entered into the mystery—at times terrifying, at times consoling—of the promise of life after death.

> Christianity asserts that every individual human being is going to live for ever, and this must be either true or false. Now there are a good many things which would not be worth bothering about if I were going to live only seventy years, but which I had better bother about very seriously if I am going to live for ever. Perhaps my bad temper or my jealousy are gradually getting worse—so gradually that the increase in seventy years will not be very noticeable. But it might be absolute hell in a million years: in fact, if Christianity is true, Hell is the precisely correct technical term for what it would be. (C. S. Lewis, *Mere Christianity*, p. 59)

Yet, Lewis was not so much plagued by the fears of hell as he was confident in the purifying and transforming acts of God that would bring about the resurrection.

On the marble plaque that Lewis commissioned for the grave of his wife, Joy, he refers to this new day.

> Here the whole world (stars, water, air,
> And field, and forest, as they were
> Reflected in a single mind)
> Like cast-off clothes was left behind
> In ashes yet with hope that she,
> Re-born from holy poverty,
> In lenten lands, hereafter may
> Resume them on her Easter Day.

Lewis himself died on 22 November 1963, after a short period of illness. His friend Austin Farrer wrote:

> The life that Lewis lived with zest he surrendered with composure. He was put almost beside himself by his wife's death; he seemed easy at the approach of his own. He died at the last in a moment. May he everlastingly rejoice in the Mercy he sincerely trusted. (Como, ed., *C. S. Lewis at the Breakfast Table*, p. 244)

The incredulity of some on hearing of his death is charmingly summed up in the case of a young boy who, upon hearing of Lewis's death, wrote him the following letter: "Dear Mr. Lewis, I'm sorry you died."

Pause: Ask yourself, Do I live in the hope of my resurrection?

Lewis's Words

God has given us the Morning Star already: you can go and enjoy the gift on many fine mornings if you get up early enough. What more, you may ask, do we want? Ah, but we want so much more—something the books on aesthetics take little notice of. But the poets and the mythologies know all about it. We do not want merely to *see* beauty, though, God knows, even that is bounty enough. We want something else which can hardly be put into words—to be united with the beauty we see, to pass into it, to receive it into ourselves, to bathe in it, to become part of it. That is why we have peopled air and earth and water with gods and goddesses and nymphs and elves— that, though we cannot, yet these projections can, enjoy in themselves that beauty, grace, and power of which Nature is the image. That is why the poets tell us such lovely falsehoods. They talk as if the west wind could really sweep into a human soul; but it can't. They tell us that "beauty born of murmuring sound" will pass into a human face; but it won't. Or not yet. For if we take the imagery of Scripture seriously, if we believe that God will one day *give* us the Morning Star and cause us to *put on* the splendour of the sun, then we may surmise that both the ancient myths and the modern poetry, so false as history, may be very near the truth as prophecy. At present we are on the outside of the world, the wrong side of the door. We discern the freshness and purity of morning, but they do not make us fresh and pure. We cannot mingle with the splendours we see. But all the leaves of the New Testament are rustling with the rumour that it will not always be so. Some day, God willing, we shall get *in*. (C. S. Lewis, *The Weight of Glory*, pp. 12–13)

Reflection

Lewis went through death's door in the hope of the Resurrection, believing that it was for him a necessary transition to greater union with God.

In Lewis's view, life after death is rooted in life before death. Life after death will not be an escape from ourselves and the good and ills of this cosmos but rather a deeper, intensified journey into God in fellowship with a redeemed creation. He thought of the afterlife as integrally related to this life, a further, mysterious stage in the person's relation to God.

Lewis's hope in life after death was built on his belief in Christ's Resurrection and its testimony of God's power and love. Because of God's power, how can we rule out an afterlife? Would this be too difficult a task for an omnipotent Creator? No act of sin, no matter how great, can impede omnipotence. As for God's love, does not love require one to long for the fulfillment of the beloved? Even in this human finite life, how can one desire that one's beloved perish when, and if, one has the power to restore this beloved to a full life? God's omnipotent love and its testimony in Christ's Resurrection grounded Lewis's faith.

Lewis suggested that we may well think that there is a natural time to die, when our bodies simply give out or we are compelled to yield to an illness or physical injury, but this does not mean that there is a natural time to perish everlastingly, to be annihilated forever or unalterably disintegrated. In death our body will return to dust; our souls are elsewhere. Christian hope and faith is in a God of abounding, profound love, a God who has power, not only to create the cosmos but to raise us up on the last day.

✧ Take time to visit a cemetery, walking slowly around the graves. Let your thoughts and feelings surface. Pray as the Spirit moves you.

✧ Listen to a recording of Handel's *Messiah*. Be particularly attentive to the trumpets when the section from First Corinthians, chapter 15, verses 51–57 is being sung.

✧ Reread the "Lewis's Words" section. Awaken your desire or recall your significant experiences when you yearned to enter into the gentleness, beauty, power, and expansiveness of life around you.

✧ Visit a garden (at any season!), and contemplate what is happening in the earth.
✦ Notice what is dying and what is coming to life.
✦ Think of what you can expect in the next few months.
✦ Apply what you have contemplated to growth and changes in your own inner life.
✦ Recite a psalm of praise as you close this time of prayer.

God's Word

Listen, I will tell you a mystery! We will not all die, but we will all be changed, in a moment, in the twinkling of an eye, at the last trumpet. For the trumpet will sound, and the dead will be raised imperishable, and we will be changed. For this perishable body must put on imperishability, and this mortal body must put on immortality. . . . Then the saying that is written will be fulfilled:

"Death has been swallowed up in victory."
"Where, O death, is your victory?
Where, O death, is your sting?"

The sting of death is sin, and the power of sin is the law. But thanks be to God, who gives us the victory through our Lord Jesus Christ. (1 Corinthians 15:51–57)

Closing prayer: O all-powerful God, may we join Christ Jesus in victory over death and in everlasting life with you. Amen.

A·L·L·E·L·U·I·A

✧ For Further Reading ✧

Selected Books by C. S. Lewis

The Chronicles of Narnia. New York: HarperCollins, 1997.

The Four Loves. New York: Harcourt, Brace and Company, 1960.

God in the Dock: Essays on Theology and Ethics. Edited by Walter Hooper. Grand Rapids, MI: William B. Eerdmans Publishing Company, 1970.

A Grief Observed. N. W. Clerk, pseudonym of C. S. Lewis. Greenwich, CT: Seabury Press, 1963.

Letters to Malcolm: Chiefly on Prayer. New York: Harcourt Brace Jovanovich, 1964.

Mere Christianity. New York: Macmillan Company, 1952.

Miracles: A Preliminary Study. New York: Macmillan Company, 1947.

The Screwtape Letters. New York: Touchstone Book, 1996.

Surprised by Joy: The Shape of My Early Life. New York: Harcourt, Brace and Company, 1955.

That Hideous Strength: A Modern Fairy-Tale for Grown-Ups. New York: Collier, 1965.

Till We Have Faces. New York: Harcourt Brace, 1984.

Books About C. S. Lewis

Green, Roger Lancelyn, and Walter Hooper. *C. S. Lewis: A Biography.* New York: Harcourt Brace Jovanovich, 1974.

Hannay, Margaret Patterson. *C. S. Lewis.* New York: Ungar, 1981.

Holmer, Paul L. *C. S. Lewis: The Shape of His Faith and Thought.* New York: Harper and Row, 1976.

Hooper, Walter. *C. S. Lewis: A Companion and Guide.* San Francisco: HarperCollins, 1996.

Howard, Thomas. *C. S. Lewis: Man of Letters.* San Francisco: Ignatius, 1987.

Kreeft, Peter. *C. S. Lewis for the Third Millennium.* San Francisco: Ignatius, 1994.

Purtill, Richard. *C. S. Lewis's Case for the Christian Faith.* San Francisco: Harper and Row, 1981.

Smith, Robert H. *Patches of Godlight: The Pattern of Thought in C. S. Lewis.* Athens, GA: University of Georgia Press, 1981.

Acknowledgments *(continued)*

The psalms in this book are from *Psalms Anew: In Inclusive Language,* compiled by Nancy Schreck and Maureen Leach (Winona, MN: Saint Mary's Press, 1986). Copyright © 1986 by Saint Mary's Press. All rights reserved.

All other scriptural quotations in this book are from the New Revised Standard Version of the Bible. Copyright © 1989 by the Division of Christian Education of the National Council of the Churches of Christ in the United States of America. All rights reserved.

The excerpts on pages 13, 24, 51, 76–77, 92, 93, 98, 101, and 106 are from *C. S. Lewis at the Breakfast Table and Other Reminiscences,* edited by James T. Como (New York: Macmillan Publishing Company, 1979), pages 125, 243, 188, 226, 21, 22, xxx, xxxiv, and 244, respectively. Copyright © 1979 by James T. Como. Used by permission of James T. Como.

The excerpts on pages 15, 23, 23, 26, 27, 75, and 105 are from *Letters of C. S. Lewis,* edited by W. H. Lewis (New York: Harcourt, Brace and World, 1966), pages 214, 141, 190, 275, 276, 248, and 3, respectively. Copyright © 1966 by W. H. Lewis and Executors of C. S. Lewis. Permission applied for.

The excerpt on page 16 is from *Perelandra: A Novel,* by C. S. Lewis (New York: Macmillan Publishing Company, 1944), page 116. Copyright © 1944 by C. S. Lewis.

The excerpts on pages 17 and 33 are from *The Pilgrim's Regress: An Allegorical Apology for Christianity, Reason and Romanticism,* by C. S. Lewis (Grand Rapids, MI: William B. Eerdmans Publishing Company, 1959), pages 10 and 156–157. Copyright © 1959 by C. S. Lewis.

The excerpts on pages 21, 52, 59, 68, 83–84, 102, and 106 are from *Mere Christianity,* by C. S. Lewis (New York: Macmillan Company, 1952), pages 31, 127, 106, 148, 52, 137, and 59, respectively. Copyright © 1943, 1945, 1952 by the Macmillan Company. Used by permission of HarperCollins Publishers, Ltd.

The excerpt on pages 34–35 is from *On Stories and Other Essays on Literature,* by C. S. Lewis, edited by Walter Hooper (New York: Harcourt Brace Jovanovich, Publishers, 1982), page 12. Copyright © 1982 by the Trustees of the Estate of C. S. Lewis.

The excerpts on pages 35–36, 51–52, and 57 are from *Letters to Malcolm: Chiefly on Prayer,* by C. S. Lewis (New York: Harcourt Brace Jovanovich, 1964), pages 88, 67–68, and 89–90, respectively. Copyright © 1963, 1964 by the Estate of C. S. Lewis. Permission applied for.

The excerpts on pages 40, 45–46, 46, 84, 87–88, 88–89, and 98–99 are from *Miracles: A Preliminary Study,* by C. S. Lewis (New York: Macmillan Company, 1947), pages 132–133, 96–97, 52–53, 161, 111–112, 116–117, and 67, respectively. Copyright © 1947 by C. S. Lewis. Permission applied for.

The excerpts on pages 42, 72, and 95 are from *Poems,* by C. S. Lewis, edited by Walter Hooper (New York: Harcourt, Brace and World, 1964), pages 98, 134, and 109–110, respectively. Copyright © 1964 by the Executors of the Estate of C. S. Lewis. Permission applied for.

The excerpt on page 45 is from *The Magician's Nephew,* by C. S. Lewis (London: The Bodley Head, 1955), page 123. Copyright © 1955 by C. S. Lewis.

The excerpt on page 47 is from *Topophilia: A Study of Environmental Perception, Attitudes, and Values,* by Yi-Fu Tuan (Englewood Cliffs, NJ: Prentice-Hall, 1974), page 96. Copyright © 1974 by Prentice-Hall.

The excerpts on pages 50 and 51 are from *The World's Last Night,* by C. S. Lewis (New York: Harcourt, Brace and Company, 1952), pages 8 and 8. Copyright © 1960 by C. S. Lewis.

The excerpt on page 54 is from *Alexandrian Christianity,* vol. 2, by John Oulton, DD, and Henry Chadwick, BD (Philadelphia: Westminster Press, 1954), page 115.

The excerpt on pages 55–56 is from *Studies in Medieval and Renaissance Literature,* by C. S. Lewis, compiled by Walter Hooper (London: Cambridge University Press, 1966), page 60. Copyright © 1966 by Cambridge University Press. Used by permission.

Titles in the Companions for the Journey Series

Praying with Anthony of Padua

Praying with Benedict

Praying with C. S. Lewis

Praying with Catherine McAuley

Praying with Catherine of Siena

Praying with Clare of Assisi

Praying with Dominic

Praying with Dorothy Day

Praying with Elizabeth Seton

Praying with Francis of Assisi

Praying with Francis de Sales

Praying with Frédéric Ozanam

Praying with Hildegard of Bingen

Praying with Ignatius of Loyola

Praying with John Baptist de La Salle

Praying with John Cardinal Newman

Praying with John of the Cross

Praying with Julian of Norwich

Praying with Louise de Marillac

Praying with Meister Eckhart

Praying with Teresa of Ávila

Praying with Thérèse of Lisieux

Praying with Thomas Merton

Praying with Vincent de Paul

Order from your local religious bookstore or from

Saint Mary's Press
702 TERRACE HEIGHTS
WINONA MN 55987-1320
USA
1-800-533-8095